Phil invites us to embark upon an epic quest to discover our meaning and purpose in life. With practical insights and a wealth of knowledge and life stories, Phil guides us on an adventure of a lifetime. You will Awaken to the design of the Creator and learn the new values and strategies you will need to Love Your Life and Live Your Legacy Today.

William W Patmon III, Patmon Law Firm, Columbus, OH.

This is a compelling model of the transformation that takes place when one becomes a committed believer in the Creator's plan for your life. Phil's story and examples make this an important book for both faith and community business alike.

Dr. Jim Augspurger, Executive Pastor, Grace at Polaris, Westerville, OH.

I believe this book will remind you of something you once believed; that you are made for more than a life of Ordinary. "Awakening! The Dreamer's Quest" is an invitation to the "more" that God has for you. Best of all, the invitation is given in an engaging and refreshingly honest way; the words of a man I know and love who has faithfully committed himself to his own God-ordained Quest. May you be blessed as you read.

Chris Ogden, Lead Pastor of Horizon West Church, Winter Garden, Fl.

I have had a courtside seat to watch Phil Johnson grow into a person committed to serving others. I have seen him at his best and I have been there with him when he needed support. Phil has been a true beacon of light to ministry leaders like me for decades... his cutting-edge insights continue to inspire True Servant Leadership as we navigate the Me Generation. "Awakening! The Dreamer's Quest in a road map to discovering your purpose in life.

Pastor Gordie Lindsay, Executive Director, His Harvest Ministries, Pontiac, Michigan

AWAKENING!

THE DREAMER'S QUEST

Five Gates That Determine Your Ultimate Purpose

Step-by-Step Guide for Loving Your Life and
Living Your Legacy Today!

PHILIP B. JOHNSON

© 2019 by Philip B. Johnson

Published by Author Academy Elite
P.O. Box 43, Powell, OH 43065
www.AuthorAcademyElite.com

Printed in the United States of America

Library of Congress Cataloging-in-Publication Data

Johnson, Philip B. 1960-

Awakening! The Dreamer's Quest: five gates that will determine your ultimate purpose: love your life and live your legacy today! / Philip B. Johnson

Softcover: ISBN 978-1-64085-596-0 (pbk.)
Hardback: ISBN 978-1-64085-597-7
Ebook: ISBN 978-1-64085-598-4

(LCCN): 2019934180

DEDICATION

To all those who have gone before me,
Who dared to Dream, believe, and do
To show the path to my Dream:
I thank you.

To my wife, Sandy,
Who dared to Dream, believe, and say "I do"
To make me the man I am today:
I love you.

I Dream, I test my Dreams against my beliefs, I dare to take risks, and I execute my vision to make those Dreams come true.

Walt Disney

***

It's not an easy road, but if the Lord has called us and put us where we are, He will see to it that we will know His will and accomplish it no matter how impossible it might seem.

Dr. Warren Wiersbe

CONTENTS

Like a Splinter in My Mind ix

Foreword xi

Introduction: The Son of a Sharecropper—
    Becoming an Extraordinary, Ordinary Man! xiii

PART 1: TO DREAM—AWAKENING! 1

1. Awakening Your Dream! The Calling of Greatness 7

2. Answering Your Dream! The Calling of Your Soul 21

3. Activating your Dream! The Calling of Total
    and Radical Commitment 33

PART 2: TO BELIEVE—ACQUIRING! 43

4. Observing Your Mind: The New Principles
    Designed for the Quest. 47

5. Observing Your Heart: The New Passion
    Meant for the Quest 58

6. Observing Your Soul: The New Purpose
    Intended for the Quest 73

PART 3: TO DARE—AFFECTING! 85

7. Dare to Discern Your Gatekeepers:
    The Well-Intentioned Critics 91

8. Deleting Your Scripts: The False Scripts We Believe . . 107

9. Dare to Diminish Detours:
    Perceiving Your Problems as Blessings in Disguise. . . . 125

PART 4: TO DO—ACTIVATING! 141

10. Awaken Your Legacy. 145

11. Accomplish Your Calling 157

12. Assemble Your Team. 169

PART 5: TO BE—ACHIEVING! 181

13. Loving Your Life and Living Your Legacy Today! 185

Acknowledgements. 195

Appendix A: Journal and Group Discussion Question . . . 199

About the author 209

LIKE A SPLINTER IN MY MIND

Tripp has a Dream.

He sits pondering a thought that is like a splinter in his mind. It has burrowed itself deep within his consciousness. Day and night, the Dream takes him beyond the borders of Ordinary. Ordinary has always been his home, even though it has never felt like home to him.

It is also the only land our traveler has ever known. He has never been outside the walls of this conventional, familiar, and mundane land. He merely exists from day to day, longing for a better life.

He spends much of his free time (that is, the time not taken up in the routine activities of Ordinary) gazing in the direction of a gate.

He wonders if it will lead to a place that is calling to his soul...

Can you feel the unfulfilled mission of your life?

Do you hear the call within your soul?

Do you have a Dream?

Are you ready to begin your adventure? Do you long for an Awakening? Will you embark upon your Dreamer's Quest?

FOREWORD

We all need answers to the big questions in life. *Who am I? Why am I here? What am I to be? Where am I to be? How will I find meaning and purpose?* My friend Phil Johnson has devoted his life to providing the answers to these universal questions.

There is a pandemic of lack of purpose.

This pandemic has spread like a cancer into every corner and stratum of society. It is not one that medicine can control or prevent. It causes devastating results in the quality of life for those who suffer from this pandemic or know someone else who does.

It is a pandemic of loss of purpose and meaning in life. A recent poll released by the Gallup Organization revealed an alarming result. It found that 55 percent of workers today are disengaged from their daily work while another 16 percent are actively disengaged. That means only 29 percent of workers today are engaged at their workplaces.

This poll reveals a deeper struggle. Many people feel like captives in prisons of their own design. They feel trapped, enslaved and dissatisfied. Yet they feel something else as well— the desire to become a "Soul on Fire." They long for freedom, fulfillment, and meaning in their lives.

In *Awakening! The Dreamer's Quest* you will discover that there has been a plan, purpose and meaning for your life from before the beginning of time. You will be guided into an adventure the Creator has designed you for.

There is a path that will lead you to the answers you long for.

Your adventure will begin as you encounter five gates that reveal and equip you to love your life and live your legacy! Phil has taken stories from his journey, the Bible, and modern "dreamers" to equip you for your Dreamer's Quest. Each gate is a passage into the process of discovering and becoming the person God designed you to be:

- To Dream—Awakening!
- To Believe—Acquiring!
- To Dare—Affecting!
- To Do—Activating!
- To Be—Achieving!

Awakening! The Dreamer's Quest will inspire you to discover your purpose. It will equip you for the battles you will face along the way. It will encourage you to become the person of your dreams. Your adventure awaits.

Kary Oberbrunner, author of *Your Secret Name, The Deeper Path, Day Job to Dream Job and Elixir Project*

INTRODUCTION

THE SON OF A SHARECROPPER—BECOMING AN EXTRAORDINARY, ORDINARY MAN!

My father, Charles Hershel Johnson, had just passed away, and I had the responsibility to speak at his funeral. I began to review the tales I had been told about my dad and the memories I had of this larger-than-life man who had just made his journey to heaven. As I began to pull my thoughts together all I could think was, *What an extraordinary, ordinary man!*

In his later years he had become a gentle, loving, and sometimes surprisingly emotional man. This was a huge departure from the man I had known in my childhood. Before I was born, he was known as a tough, stubborn, quick-tempered, hard man. His early life had been equally hard and tough, which had made him stubborn and ill tempered. He grew up with an absentee father, raised by a mother who showed little love or affection. He only made it through the eighth grade. His life's path would be altered.

During his later childhood and early teen years, his mother provided for their family by moving between Tennessee and Michigan to harvest crops as a migrant worker. It was the

Great Depression and talk of war filled the air. His mother finally decided that the family could no longer shoulder the burden of feeding and housing my dad. They would have to send him away.

My father was sent to a CCC Camp in Wisconsin. CCC stood for Civilian Conservation Corps, which was part of President Roosevelt's New Deal program to give a leg up to those in need during the Great Depression. Dad lived in the barracks and worked lining highways with fences until he lied about his age to join the U.S. Navy. He served four years during the latter part of World War II, securing safe access for shipping through the Panama Canal by keeping enemy submarines from crossing between the Atlantic and Pacific Oceans.

While on leave during the Christmas holidays, my dad visited a young lady he had been writing to. Somehow, during a weeklong uninvited stay at my mom's house in Tennessee, he managed to meet her, court her, and convince her to marry him. The day after Christmas, they slipped away to Jackson, Mississippi to get married. (The laws in Mississippi were well-suited for a teen sneaking off and getting married without her father's permission.) He then moved my mom to Miami, Florida. They had a small apartment, and my mom worked in a diner near the greyhound racing track.

After serving four years in the Navy, my dad was discharged. He and my mom moved from Miami to a small farm in western Tennessee nestled near Trenton, Humboldt and Milan to sharecrop with my mom's father. Farming proved to be more than my dad had bargained for. With the prospects of a failing crop and mounting debts, Dad had to seek employment at the local munitions factory to care for his growing family. My mom also went to work in the same factory.

However, Dad didn't last very long there in the plant. He was let go due to union activity. His efforts to form a union at the Milan Arsenal was not met with approval by its owners.

In 1950 in the South, business owners viewed unions as a bunch of troublemakers who had no place in any company. He was let go.

Dad was still farming as a sharecropper, but the harvest did not appear to be good enough to cover everything that was due. Each fall the rent for the small farmhouse, rent for the farmland where he had planted a crop of cotton, and payment for last spring's seed and any food they had bought on credit all came due. Knowing the cotton crop was sure to fail, and they would never get enough to cover these expenses, Dad packed up my mom and two older brothers into a pickup truck and moved to Pontiac, Michigan. (In my family the 1960's sitcom *The Beverly Hillbillies* was a bit too close to reality to be all that funny!)

Other family members from Tennessee had moved to Pontiac to find work in the automobile factories, so my family stayed with them. Dad stood in line at the employment office of General Motors Truck and Coach and was given a job on the assembly line.

This allowed my father and mother to start anew: not only to earn a living, but to pay back every penny they owed in Tennessee. First, they lived with family, then rented a couple of houses, and eventually had the means to purchase a house for $9,000 with a monthly payment of $78. This was a huge investment for them.

A few years before I was born, my dad began to attend church. Not only did he attend church, but he also became a totally and radically committed follower of Jesus Christ. Not only did we attend every service—which included Sunday School, Sunday morning and evening services and Wednesday Night prayer meeting—but Dad also attended Thursday night calling and made Saturday-morning visits to each child he would pick up and return home on his Sunday morning church bus route. My dad became a leader in the church and soon was on the deacon board. We made a change in churches when I was ten years old, and we were just as committed to our new church.

Dad's relationship with Jesus Christ transformed him slowly over the years. He began to read books about missionaries, Christian doctrine and Christian living just about every night. His commitment to studying the Bible became a habit that he remained faithful to 'til the end of his life. Most years, Dad would read the entire Bible cover to cover.

His relationship with Jesus also provided a path to the first stable home he had ever known. When he and my mom were able to purchase a 777 square foot house for their family of four, it was the first safe place for both of my parents. (This would be the only home I would know until I moved to college many years later. But I'm getting ahead of myself here.) His journey from a childhood of moving around, to life in a CCC camp and the Navy, to a tenant shack in Tennessee, to finally building a new house, was extraordinary. The size of the house did not match the size of the transformation.

Then I arrived on the scene. I guess my arrival was the talk of the neighborhood! My brothers were fourteen and twelve upon my arrival. They had morning and evening paper routes for about 500 houses in the neighborhood. Because my mom and dad felt they were too old to be parents of a new baby, they tried to keep my arrival a secret. But when my brothers found out they made it their mission to share this news with everybody as they delivered papers. It was 1960 and you just didn't share that type of news to just anyone, especially if you had celebrated your thirtieth birthday already. My mom never forgave them for that one.

I grew up in the '60s and '70s as a son of a sharecropper in a city that knew nothing about my background. It was the Age of Aquarius, man! Although my dad's strict parenting tampered my *total* engagement in the counterculture, I was much like any other young person growing up in that era. In the 1970s, young people would question authority and try to find themselves. The counterculture wanted to sit in the park, get high and play Frisbee. It was cool to be anti-everything other than love, sex, and drugs.

Our generation was a true paradox. On one hand, we had tremendous passion and turmoil that boiled within our souls. There was a longing for something inside us, but we didn't know how to express those feelings maturely. Then, on the other side of the equation, we couldn't care less. So, I grew up with a whole generation that was angry, frustrated, seeking, and longing for better times, but didn't want to endure the pain it would take to earn it. We had Dreams without any clarity, competence, or confidence.

But let's get back to my dad's story. Over the next few decades Dad became a loving man of God. He pursued his passions. He took up running while I was on the cross-country team in high school and college. My dad was at just about every sporting event I ever participated in, and many of the practices, too.

He became a very good runner for his age, winning many medals and trophies. He started a couple of businesses after retiring in 1982 from General Motors. In retirement he bought two more houses, both of which were built just for him and mom. He also took up bowling—but after he bowled his third 300 game, he gave it up because it wasn't a challenge anymore. He then took up golf, but he was never able to conquer *that* game. Retirement also allowed Dad to assist in starting a church in Florida that is now a megachurch. He also was an evangelist to the day he died, sharing the gospel of Jesus Christ to everyone he met. And, as far as I know, he read through the Bible every year until his death. (I have the worn Bibles to prove it.)

It was the winter of 2006 that I received a call from one of my brothers that Mom and Dad were in a bad car accident in northern Michigan. I needed to come quickly.

As I made my way north, my mind was filled with the memories of my life. I was successful by many measures. I had a great wife, kids, and job. Owned a beautiful house. Was the first college graduate in my family. I'd even taken courses in several different advanced degree programs.

But none of that brought me comfort when I learned that the accident had done irreparable damage to my father's body. I had prepared myself for that news, but I wasn't prepared to learn that Dad had an aggressive, fast-moving cancer that had moved into just about every organ in his body. His time was very short.

Somebody needed to tell Dad. Almost in unison, my family and the doctors agreed that it should be me. I was overwhelmed with grief, but I couldn't show it now. I had to be strong for my dad, my mom, and my family. How was I going to tell this man, who had become my hero, that he was going to leave this world?

As I stood by Dad's hospital bed, I looked into his clouded blues eyes. I wondered if he already knew. He seemed to always know things before I ever spoke a word.

"Dad, how are you doing?"

"Oh, I'm okay. How was your trip? It's good to see you, son."

"I'm okay, Dad. But the news isn't too good for you."

"Oh?"

"The doctors say you're going home to heaven soon, Dad…"

"Oh boy, that's great! Get the grandkids here, son. I want to talk to them!"

And with that, he started to close up shop. For several days I listened to my dad say good-bye to family members and friends. I heard an excitement in his voice for the journey he was about to make, but a sadness that he had to take the journey alone. He'd always believed and hoped that we would all meet Jesus together when He returned for His followers. I guess that's one of the reasons he took the news of his departure so well. He was ready.

I've spent more time thinking about my dad's life and how he reacted to it coming to an end than any other moments in my life. How in the world did my dad take this news so well? How was he so ready to move forward? Where did he get such clarity of purpose?

While my quest to find meaning in my life had begun many years before, my dad's reaction to only having a few days left brought great clarity to me. I could see that I needed to pursue my quest with the same passion I saw in my dad's life. He had squeezed a lifetime of dreams into the last twenty-five years of his life. It became clear to me that I must pursue with passion the dreams I had set aside from many years prior. I was having an Awakening—or, should I say, a re-Awakening! Just like dad, I was now determined to begin a Dreamer's Quest of my own. The same Quest that my father was finishing in such a spectacular fashion.

Dad had found a secret I had been looking for my whole life! He had lived his passion and loved his life during his last years on earth. He had become what he was designed to be. He had no regrets, because he had fulfilled his Dream. He had discovered how to love his life by being the man God had designed him to be.

I want that! To be able to say, "Oh boy, that's great!" when I receive my call to heaven.

That is what *Awakening! The Dreamer's Quest* is all about. It is about setting your life course to reach that Dream, that longing, that pain deep within you. It is about the new rules that you must follow to reach your destination: The Dream Within. It is also about the battles you must face and the enemies you must defeat to stay on course. Finally, it is about making the Dream reality—loving your life and living your legacy today!

It is an honor to embark alongside you on your very own Dreamer's Quest. While your Dream may look different from mine, your Quest will be the same. I look forward to guiding you through this adventure of a lifetime! While it may not always be fun, it will thrill your soul and give rise to discovery of your person, purposes, and passions.

I must warn you now, this may be the hardest journey you've ever set out on—but it will also be the most important one! In the words of Tom Hanks in the movie *A League of Their Own* when confronted by his all-star catcher, Dotty Henson with how hard it was to be a professional female baseball player, "It's supposed to be hard. If it was easy, everybody would do it."

Are you ready for adventure? Are you ready for passion? Are you ready for the rewards that come from embarking on a journey to discovery that Dream hidden within your soul and to become the person the Creator has designed you to be? Then let's get started!

PART 1

TO DREAM—AWAKENING!

Tripp senses there is more to his life than the mundane drudgery that the citizens of Ordinary endure each day.

The reappearing apparition of a veiled Dream haunts him day and night. Is there a Dream that can transport his spirit beyond the borders of this existence? Ordinary has always been his home, though this place has never felt like home to him. He has never been outside the walls of this conventional, familiar, and mundane land. He merely exists from day to day, longing for a better life. He spends much of his free time (that is, the time not taken up in the routine activities of Ordinary) gazing in the direction of a gate that leads away from this realm. He wonders if it will lead him to the place that is calling his spirit away.

One day, Tripp notices a Traveler moving with purpose and great speed through Ordinary. The Traveler stands out from the other citizens of Ordinary. In Ordinary, people move about slowly, as they retrace the same paths each day. Most wear masks to conceal their pain, but their eyes always give them away.

However, the Traveler is moving with singular purpose and direction. She does not follow any of the patterns of the others. Tripp notices that she does not wear a mask, and that she has an unusually pleasant look about her. It appears she is moving *through* Ordinary, against the normal routines. She moves with a single-mindedness, a resolve, and a persistence that irritates most of the citizens of Ordinary.

Tripp is intrigued and drawn to interrupt her march through Ordinary. He must get an answer to the burning question that haunts his soul. *She seems to know where she's going—and, more importantly, why. What does she know that I don't?* Tripp wonders to himself.

They speak as strangers who have just crossed paths, and Tripp expresses great interest about where she is heading and why she is going there.

"To my Dream," she responds matter-of-factly.

"Dream? What—where—what do you mean?" Tripp inquires.

"I have been made for a purpose, a reason. You could say it is my 'calling.' I have a part to play in the grand scheme of things that is very important. I am making my way to fulfill that role so others can benefit from the gifts that are entrusted to me." While the tone of the Traveler is very direct and to-the-point, her words seem to have a deeper meaning that Tripp does not grasp in the moment. "How can I help you?" she asks.

"Oh, I just saw you and I didn't recognize you. I could tell that you are not from h—"

Tripp is cut off by the Traveler. "Oh, I'm from here, but it is not my home. It never really *was* my home. You are seeking answers. It sounds like you should check out the land beyond the gate that is close by. I am heading there now. You will find answers to your questions beyond that gate."

She points to the gate that has captured Tripp's imagination many times before. After a brief pause of what looks like a moment of gratitude and remembrance, she continues, "I have found great clarity in the land beyond that gate."

With that, the Traveler turns and moves towards the gate. Tripp follows her into an area of Ordinary where he has seldom traveled. Very few who live in Ordinary dare to approach the area because of the tales of citizens who have entered the gate and never returned home. There are a few abandoned, makeshift shacks that look like temporary houses for people passing through. But there isn't much of the usual types of activity and routine you would find in the more popular centers of Ordinary. Tripp has heard stories about The Travelers, but he had not believed the wild stories of great adventures these fabled people had been upon. Unsure of himself because he has left his normal patterns, he allows the Traveler to move ahead and slip through the doors of the huge gate.

Tripp has only seen this gate from a distance. Now he stands in awe before this massive structure. When she is almost out of view, the Traveler looks back over her shoulder, smiles, and gives a quick motion of a beckoning, openhanded wave for Tripp to follow in her footsteps.

Tripp stops at the opening of the huge gate. Peering through the opening, Tripp can see that just beyond the entrance, there is a path into a vast, unknown land. He can see clearly for miles. The sights he views remind him of shadowy images he has had glimpses of in his solitary moments of yearning for an escape from Ordinary. Something is stirred within his soul. So profound is this moment that he will later refer to it as his Awakening!

Tripp returns to Ordinary, only to be preoccupied by the encounter with the Traveler and the sights of the land beyond the gate. He not only returns there in his thoughts, but he also revisits the entrance of the gate to learn more and to reconnect with the stirring deep within his soul that he doesn't understand. Tripp has a sense that this is the path to discover more about the calling of his Dream. Each time he draws close to this mysterious gate, he gains new insights to the passions of his heart.

He finds himself standing before the large gate, examining and pondering his choices: to remain, or to embark on a Quest for his Dream. The gate looks much like what you would imagine guarding heaven. But here it is, right in from of him.

Tripp takes note of the word written in bold letters above the gate: *Dream*.

Dream Gate, that's an interesting name, he thinks to himself. Upon closer examination, he discovers written upon the doors an inscription: *To See with Clarity*. Tripp remembers the words of the Traveler. It is then that he realizes that the walls surround Ordinary, and not the land before him. True freedom is only found on the other side of this gate and can never be found within the limits of Ordinary.

After these discoveries, Tripp decides to examine the other side of the gate. As he passes through the gate, it opens onto a vast overlook. He can see roads and paths that appear to lead to several more gates. Behind each gate he can see what appears to be monuments that Travelers had placed left there while passing through to the lands of each of the gates. Only in his imagination had a place like this existed.

Immediately in front of him, he can see a land that he has always known was there, but that he could never see from the other side of the wall surrounding Ordinary. He lingers here at the entrance, only to return to Ordinary after just a moment of consideration. The draw of adventure will call him back on many occasions. However, he retreats to the "safety" of Ordinary each time.

Today is different. The longing and the call beyond the Dream Gate builds up his courage to inch his way through to the first crossroads. He stands in quiet thought as he examines the paths that stretch before him. The possibilities of discovery and adventure thrill his soul.

Then, just as suddenly as hope has filled his soul, a wave of fear overtakes him. He turns and retreats to the cloudy, muddy existence of the mundane life within Ordinary. Back within the confines of Ordinary, he finds himself thinking about the feeling of hope he has experienced. He wonders if he can replace his fear with hope. Could he possess the hope he found in Ordinary as his own? Could he fill the festering hole within his soul?

Tripp returns many times, sometimes even setting up a camp and staying at the crossroads overnight. Somehow, while camping there at the crossroads, he feels more connected to the Dream that stirs deep within his soul. But, during these overnight stays, he makes sure to always keep the huge Dream Gate in sight, so he can peer back into the city of Ordinary. He has always known Ordinary as home, and he believes it is the only safe place to be. During each of these stays, it does not take long for the responsibilities of Ordinary to draw him back into their routines. Again, he retreats within the walls, where he feels safety. But with that safety comes a deep feeling of dissatisfaction.

Tripp, being determined to uncover the secrets of the land beyond the Dream Gate, plans an extended stay to explore the land. During this expedition, while experiencing the challenges of leaving the safety and the duties of Ordinary, Tripp begins to encounter himself in an honest and illuminating fashion. Away from the noise of Ordinary, he can hear with clarity the voice that had been reverberating within him. He discovers it is the Creator's voice that had been calling to him all along. The Creator softly reassures him that he is loved, he is special, and that he has a very important gift to share with the world.

Tripp learns that this is where travelers are confronted by the Creator and His design for them. Along with that design, they become aware of a grand Quest He has planned for them. Travelers to this place gain clarity to see their Dream and find the path to their true purpose, passion, and calling. The travelers also discover their identity and meaning in life. The hole within their soul becomes filled to overflowing.

Tripp comes to realize that the answers he seeks are to be found by answering life's most mystifying questions: *Who am I? Why am I here? What am I to do? How am I to live?* It is in this land that he discovers the truth about himself and charts the Quest the Creator has for him. The Dream Gate has become the jumping- off point for an adventure of a lifetime.

Tripp has an Awakening! He has awakened to the Dream within his soul. He now is faced with a decision. To commit to his Dream given to him by the Creator, or to return to Ordinary once and for all.

Tripp is determined to begin his quest, the Dreamer's Quest. He finally makes the total and radical commitment to follow this Quest wherever it may lead. In that moment of commitment, Tripp discovers even deeper meaning and calling for his life. For the very first time, Tripp feels real joy coming from within his soul. A sense of satisfaction and refreshment overtakes him. He has come in sync with his meaning and purpose, as he begins his new journey with the Creator at his side.

1

AWAKENING YOUR DREAM!
THE CALLING OF GREATNESS

When the world becomes a fantasy
And you're more than you could ever be
'Cause you're dreaming with your eyes wide open
And you know you can't go back again
To the world that you were living in
'Cause you're dreaming with your eyes wide open
So, come alive!

"Come Alive" by Hugh Jackman
(from *The Greatest Showman*)

* * *

Children get asked all kinds of questions that don't make any sense to them. I enjoy watching children's reaction to grown-up questions. Here's one I like to ask: "What do you do for a living?"

I usually get a funny look, and then some deep thought. You can tell it's the first time they've encountered this question. Mom and child exchange glances. A smile usually comes over the child's face. Then I always get this answer:

"Play."

Mom and Dad laugh. Dad begins calculating the cost of raising a child who does not produce an income but rather a regular *outflow* of cash for entertainment, toys and activities. Mom begins dreaming of what she wants her child to do for a living. The child is content with giving me the right answer—to which I say, "That's great work if you can find it. Keep that job as long as you can!"

Isn't that everybody's dream: to play all day, every day? I am sure your dream is not to labor endless hours at tasks you are ill-fitted for, that extract every ounce of energy from you. The wisdom of a child to answer "Play!" when it is really the only right answer. If we all would do that one thing in life that we love to do and we are great at, how much happier would we all be?

Most of us ask the same question in a different way: "What do you want to be when you grow up?"

This question is like nails on a chalkboard to teens. As they leave their parents' homes and their colleges to enter adulthood, we ask them the same question. It's just worded a little differently: "What do you want to do with your life?"

There doesn't seem to be a right answer. If a teen or young adult had the nerve to answer "Play!" to either question, we would call them a dreamer. If they answer with, "I want to make as much money as I can (whether it's working in the automobile factory or becoming a brain surgeon)!" we'd give them a lecture about how money isn't everything. If they answer with "I want to just be me (whether that is an artist, a writer, an actor or a racecar driver)!" we would give them the "But you can't play your life away" lecture.

As a child I wanted to play pro sports. Little did I know, that would guide me to my calling in life. The same was true of my dreams to be a forest ranger and an air traffic controller. All three gave me insight to the "What will you be when you grow up?" question.

While I went through my pro ball phase, my older brothers were quick to taunt me. They would remind me that I couldn't beat them at any sport, so how could I become pro at anything? And of course, at the time, it seemed an impossible task. (You have to have older brothers to understand that one.) I could never be as good as my brothers at anything. *I have no chance at this dream,* I thought. *I guess I'll have to pass.*

Next came the park ranger phase. After a family road trip from Michigan to California, where we visited several national parks and forests, I thought maybe I could be a park ranger. However, my imagination ran wild with fears of being outsmarted by a couple of cartoon bears. That made me second-guess *that* career move. Plus, I love being with people, and the life of a park ranger sounded lonely. After a little thought, I said, "Sorry!" to Yogi and Boo Boo.

Then there was the air traffic controller phase. In college, I heard somewhere that air traffic controllers only worked twenty-five to thirty hours a week. After a little research in the library (the Google of my youth), I learned that air traffic controllers *do* work forty hours a week, but they only work for one-and-a-half to two hours at a time with mandatory breaks. I like breaks, so that sounded cool! Especially when I learned how much they made a year. I changed my mind after I saw the movie *Airplane*, though. The pressure of tracking and ordering twenty to thirty aircraft . . . no thanks! I couldn't even navigate Pac-Man away from the four ghosts! How could I keep twenty jets flying in the right direction?

You know, it's funny, now that I think about it, that a bit of sibling rivalry, some cartoon characters, and a 1980 comedy movie helped shape my future. But it really wasn't that simple. The endless internal conversations about what I should do with my life were exhausting. There had to be a reason for me to be here. What was it?

I knew there was something deep inside me that I had to discover. It was like a splinter in my mind. Somehow, I had to discover what it meant. It was just beyond my reach. I would catch glimpses of it through the fog of life. I had just enough information to keep me searching, but not enough to draw a sharp conclusion.

I needed to answer the first question we all must answer, *Who am I?* To begin a journey, you must start with a point of reference. You must determine where you are now to determine the correct path to where you want to go. I've watched way too many Dreamers embark on their Quests, only to find themselves lost from the very beginning. They haven't taken the time to see where they're starting from. Passion without clarity of purpose leads to confusion, frustration, and failure.

Too many times we allow pain to motivate our actions without understanding our identity. To discover why we are here right now is to understand the Dreamer's Quest. That "why" will keep us on track toward our Dream.

* * *

"Look, here comes the Dreamer." That's what Joseph's brothers said when they saw him in the distance. This story of the salvation of an entire tribe is instructive to our Awakening to the Dreamer's Quest.

God had given Joseph a dream. At least that was Joseph's story. But the dream caused mistrust and confusion in the family. The dream seemed to indicate that one day Joseph would rule over his brothers and parents—that they would bow down to him in service.

This dream Joseph had dug up all the dirty family secrets of deceit, withholding of love and questioning of each other's motives—all the things we sweep under the rug.

Joseph's father, Jacob, was once known for his deceitful schemes (and, yes, even traitorous behavior). He deceived his father, Isaac. He defrauded his older brother, Esau, out of the family fortune and the blessing that was to be passed down from Abraham to the oldest son.

Joseph's grandmother, Rebekah, instructed Jacob to cheat his brother Esau out of his inheritance. Not only did she put the idea into his head, she helped with the plan.

Joseph's grandfather on his mother's side, Laban, was a real operator too. He cheated Joseph's father out of seven years of hard labor. He was a great hustler to put one over on Jacob who tricked both his father and brother.

Talk about a dysfunctional family! Joseph came from a family filled with schemers and cheats. It's no wonder his stepbrothers didn't trust him. This family had real issues with trust.

Joseph came from a blended family. Of his ten step brothers, four were from Leah, two were from Zilpah (who was Leah's slave), and two were from Bilhah (who was Rachel's slave). While Jacob had twelve sons, he only had Joseph and Benjamin with Rachel. She was the wife he loved, and Joseph and Benjamin were the sons he favored. And it was well-known that Joseph was Dad's favorite. The Bible tells us that Joseph's ten older brothers hated him.

At age seventeen, Joseph's Awakening came to him in the form of two dreams. Both seemed to have the same meaning. According to the dreams, the whole family would one day bow down to him. This included his father, his mother, and his eleven brothers (ten of whom were older step-brothers). Joseph and his younger brother were from a different wife, and one of the other three mothers was a sister to their mom. This was already a powder keg that only needed a small spark to blow. Joseph's dreams were just the thing to push the ten older brothers into action.

Joseph stood before his family sharing the Dream that God had given him. He was in search of meaning, trying to make sense of this calling upon his life. In his confusion, he was met with rejection from his older brothers.

But to be questioned by his father, who loved him more than the other brothers, I'm sure was beyond comprehension. Joseph found himself neither knowing nor understanding the Dream God had given him. Only knowing that this message was from God, Joseph was left to either accept or reject the identity God had given him.

Little did he know, events would soon unfold that would alter his life forever. Joseph would soon realize his life was out of his control. He had been given a Dream that would commence his Quest. Soon Joseph's life would be changed when his brothers sold him into slavery. While this did not look anything like the bowing of his brothers to him, it would prove to be the first step toward achieving the Dream God had given him. He must have questioned his identity and the purpose of being sold into slavery. But he held onto the Dream given to him by God.

Can you give a detailed account of who you are and what your purpose is today?

Can you describe the details of your Dream? Does your Dream confuse you?

Do you even believe it is possible to know the answers to these questions?

To find the answer to these questions, you must come to grips with how you fit into that cosmic question: where did all this come from?

Understanding where you are starting from gives you much greater clarity to understand what direction you must go. When embarking on The Dreamer's Quest, it is helpful to have an understanding about the origin of the voice within. Personally, I find my favorite book, the Bible, gives the best answers to questions about my purpose and meaning. It gives me great confidence and clarity knowing that I have been designed for a specific purpose.

You may seek answers from differing places. No worries. The truths I share in this book are time-tested by people of all walks and faiths. I share in this book the Hero's Journey, the story that is written upon each of our hearts, the same story line we use to tell our epic stories. Truth—all truth; the truth about me and about you—is found outside, above and beyond each of us.

Before any of "this" ever existed, God decided to create the universe. That is what Genesis 1:1 tells us the origin of everything is: *"In the beginning, God created the heavens and the earth."*

However, this was not the first act of creation. Like any inventor or engineer today that creates something new and different, the first act of creation takes place in the mind of the creator. The purpose and plans were drawn up before the creation act of Genesis 1:1. In fact Genesis 1:1 was the second act of creation—to bring these plans out of the mind of God and into existence in the physical world. Consider what the Bible says about the planning that took place before Genesis 1:1:

- Wisdom was established (Prov. 8:23)

- Eternal life was promised (Titus 1:2)

- Christ was foreordained (1 Pet. 1:20; Rev.13:8)

- Unrevealed secrets of God existed (Matt. 25:34)

So, what if this is true? What difference does it make for us today?

There was not only a plan for the creation of the world, but there was also a plan for every person that ever walked or will walk the face of the earth as well. There are two massive ideas in Psalm 139 that will help you understand your story and the story of every person to ever live!

Let's examine Psalm 139:13-16 to see if we can find the foundation of our story there:

¹³ For you created my inmost being;
  you knit me together in my mother's womb.
¹⁴ I praise you because I am fearfully and wonderfully made;
  your works are wonderful,
  I know that full well.
¹⁵ My frame was not hidden from you
  when I was made in the secret place,
  when I was woven together in the depths of the earth.
Psalm 139:13-15

Did you catch that? Not only has God created your inmost being—the real you—but He has also "knit" and "woven" you together before your birth. I believe this is a direct reference to how God took the available DNA and clicked every detail of your genetic make-up into place. Ponder that one for a moment.

This would mean that God not only pulled together *your* genetic code, but also the genetic code of your parents, their parents, and so on all the way back to the first man and woman. No random selection, but purposeful creation. It makes the long lists of names in the opening chapters of Matthew and Luke come alive when you realize that this planning was not limited to Jesus and his bloodline, but also includes you! God designed you with purpose, *on* purpose!

As we wonder at this act of personal creation, King David reveals another marvelous truth that has great meaning for all of us today!

¹⁶ Your eyes saw my unformed body;
  all the days ordained for me were written in your book
  before one of them came to be. Psalms 139:16

God not only saw the potential of your unformed body in its fullness, but He also wrote down your story in His book before you ever lived one day of your life. He placed you, and me, center stage in our stories written just for us!

Not only did God create you personally, He created you for purpose and meaning. He created your stage—your story—and He wrote a script just for you!

Now, as we reflect on these amazing truths, let me ask you a couple of questions:

- *Does God create things that are good or things that are bad?* God created you—personally. That means He created who you are, your identity. Just a quick scan of Genesis Chapter One would tell you that God's creative actions were good, and then very good, when He created man and woman. Certainly, we can take something good and twist it for evil, but the building materials are there for good.

- *Does God create things to succeed or to fail?* God gave you purpose and meaning. God's purpose for you is a path to success and to seeing His good and perfect will fulfilled. Once again, we can take a life marked for success and mar it with failure. However, even then, God can somehow restore that life and work it out for good (Rom. 8:28).

- *Does God love you and have your best interests at heart?* The most famous verse in our times, John 3:16, tells us that God loves us no matter what and that He has a plan to redeem us. He is offering all of this as a gift to each of us. We can enter into that perfect plan He has designed for each of us.

To See with Clarity what your Dream is, you must first See with Clarity who the author of your Dream is. He is the Creator. He loves you. He has a personal plan for you. That plan is for you to experience a personal relationship with Him. He created you personally by designing you with the exact gifts so you could step center stage of your story. He designed you to make an impact in the world today. He has programmed you to do great things! While your story may be very different from mine, it is still a story of greatness. All you need to do is Awaken to the reality that surrounds you today!

* * *

When I was a boy, I would sit in our backyard under a maple tree and dream while being wide awake:

- I would dream about being a hero for the Detroit Tigers or the Detroit Pistons. I would be a leader on my team, making big plays and leading my team to win the championship.

- I would dream of being a park ranger and come to the rescue. Maybe I would jump into a fire zone in Yosemite National Park to fight a forest fire. Or maybe I would recue hikers lost in Grand Canyon National Park. Or help capture a grizzly bear in a populated area and release him into the backcountry of Yellowstone National Park.

- I would dream of being an air traffic controller. I would guide seekers to find their way in life, much like an air traffic controller guides jets in for a landing. I could be like Ben Sliney, whose first day as the United States Federal Aviation Administration Operations Manager was September 11, 2001 (what we now call 9/11). His first day he ordered and oversaw the closure of U.S. airspace, landing thousands of jets in a little over two hours.

I had other dreams like teaching and inspiring people to transformation like Billy Graham, Zig Ziglar and other pastors and speakers I had heard. I pictured standing in front of a group, telling a story, and watching their faces light up as a transformation took hold of their lives.

Then I would snap out of my dream. I would take inventory of who I saw myself to be. I saw an ugly, skinny, kind-of-dumb kid who had very few friends and very limited resources. I was the son of a sharecropper. My dad only had an eighth grade education and worked in an automobile assembly plant. I wasn't great at sports or school. I wasn't even a very good Christian. I didn't see any path out of Pontiac, Michigan. I was stuck.

My thoughts were focused on a negative self-imagine I had created for myself and a self-fulfilling prophecy of failure I had written into my story. I needed an Awakening to God's potential He had hardwired into my DNA and the plan for my life story He had already written for me. I had heard all the right stuff about God. And even though I had a personal relationship with Jesus, it didn't seem to help much. I was left with my questions and with answers of my own making.

I was having fleeting moments of Awakening! But they were just that—fleeting. Like Joseph, who just got short clips of his Quest, I had only brief moments of imagines of doing something meaningful and important. It was not until I had an encounter with my Creator beyond the gate named Dream that I began to see with clarity the full vision God had in mind for me.

I will describe that encounter in the next chapter. For now, I was Awakened to the possibility of a fantastic journey that God had me on. The "glimpses" I had were clear—but, like Joseph, my life didn't seem to match the Dream I had received. I feared sharing any of this with others. How could it ever become a reality?

To this day, I still struggle with the little boy who sat under the maple tree. Slipping back into negative beliefs, I must remind myself of my identity and purpose. I must renew my mind daily to be reset on the fact that I was designed by

God for greatness and that I was designed to win! While it may not look like success to outsiders, God's creation is good.

Today I know that God has a personal plan for me. Second Peter 1:3 says, "For His divine power has given us everything required for life and godliness, through the knowledge of Him who called us by His own glory and goodness." All I must do is trust Him and embark on the Dreamer's Quest laid out before me each day. Like Joseph, there was a time when I did not see how any of my Dream would work out. I was just awakening to see the possibilities God had in store for me.

I struggled to understand the Dream planted with me. It almost felt more like a curse than a blessing. Part of understanding my Dream was to see that God had a plan and the means to make that plan work. I now understand the words of Paul in Romans 8:28. I had my doubts about God growing up. He seemed to be a grumpy old man in the sky who enjoyed telling me "No!" all the time.

I had a very hard time understanding that God was on my side, not against me. The idea that nothing could separate me from the love of God had not become part of my belief system. Learning that I was more than a conqueror—I was part of the family of God and my outcome is secure—blew up all my beliefs about myself.

31 What, then, shall we say in response to these things? If God is for us, who can be against us? [...] 35 Who shall separate us from the love of Christ? Shall trouble or hardship or persecution or famine or nakedness or danger or sword? [...]

37 No, in all these things we are more than conquerors through him who loved us. 38 For I am convinced that neither death nor life, neither angels nor demons neither the present nor the future, nor any powers,39 neither height nor depth, nor anything else in all creation, will be able to separate us from the love of God that is in Christ Jesus our Lord. Romans 8:31, 35, 37-39

This Quest that some will choose to embark upon has its moments of hardship and challenge. But when you see with clarity, observe with competence, and master with confidence, you will love your life and you will live your legacy today!

Like me, you must start with clarity of vision about who you really are, what you are here for, where your journey is taking you, why you are on this journey, and how you are going to get it done. The answers are simple if you stop to think about them.

- *Who am I?* A divine creation of God.

- *What am I here for?* To live in the enjoyment of doing that which God designed you to do.

- *Where is this journey taking me?* Within the story written for you by God.

- *Why am I taking this journey?* To discover the life you are designed to live.

- *How do I achieve my calling?* Confession to God, belief in your heart, and enabling of the Holy Spirit.

That's it, the secret that my dad found and lived with passion in his last days on earth. The same secret that I have been pursuing for decades now.

Your Awakening awaits! You have a choice before you. You can keep moving forward, or you can go back into the slumber of the Dreamless.

The Awakening is not the journey . . . it is only the invitation to begin the journey!

* * *

THE DREAMER'S JOURNAL

Walt Disney questioned his Dream on several occasions. My guess is that this started as a boy when he got into trouble for painting cartoon characters on the side of his father's barn, or when he turned in artwork for a failing grade in school because he drew faces on his sunflowers. Or maybe it was when the newspaper editor that said he had no talent as an artist.

During his early adult life, he failed to get a successful business model to build his Dream upon. In fact, it would be his fifth attempt before he would see success. Along with his brother Roy, he started The Disney Brother's Studio, which later became The Walt Disney Company. Before this, Walt Disney faced the rejection of his ideas, failure of his companies, theft of his intellectual property, health issues, discouragement, and depression.

But there was a Dream within his soul that kept him pursuing his passion. Many quotes about Dreams are attributed to him. Here are two:

If you can Dream it, you can do it.

All our Dreams can come true, if we have the courage to pursue them.

2

ANSWERING YOUR DREAM!
THE CALLING OF YOUR SOUL

*The meaning of life. The wasted years of life. The poor choices
of life. God answers the mess of life with one word: "grace."*

Max Lucado

* * *

As I Awakened to the idea that God has something
special in mind for my life, I wondered if I was the
only one. Although the movie *The Truman Show*
was decades away, I pondered if everybody around me knew
something about life that I didn't. My desire to know the truth
caused me to question everything. I longed for somebody to
tell me the secret to life. I was confused, struggling, and knew
I needed help.

I was prone to long monologues with God, which consisted
of me verbalizing my need for answers. Some might call this
"prayer." I would now use the term "complaining." At times it
was superficial, and at times it was heartfelt, from the core of
my being. My complaints to God continued into my teenage

year and moved more to my commentary. I would make my case something along these lines:

God, I want a really hot girlfriend. Oh yeah, if you could throw in a hot car and enough money to have a good time, too, that would be great.

You know I want to serve you, God, but I don't know what that means exactly. I do know that I don't want to end up in Africa with the Pygmies. Okay, if we could take "being a missionary" off the list, that would be great—and "school teacher and "pastor," and "going to Bible college." You know I want to have a good time!

How about I go to college and have a good time and get married, and we can investigate this whole "serving You" bit after I've had my fun. I know you have something special planned for my life, but I'm not sure about You or Your plans for me. If You could just give me a detailed outline of what life would look like in Your service, then I can get back to You with my answer.

But I really do want to do something big with my life—for You, of course—someday!

Beneath those desires of youth, I was aware of the importance of responding to the calling of my soul. It haunted me day and night. I would catch myself wondering if these ideas I had about my future were just flashes of arrogance and pride, or if they were a glimpse of what God had in mind for my future.

I had moments of future memories (or what you might call daydreams) of me leading young people in events and activities. I could see myself speaking on a stage in front of a crowd, giving inspiration and motivation. I saw lives being transformed. I saw my name on a book jacket. I had fleeting sights of myself in boardrooms, speaking and being listened to by a group of leaders. But all of this was in a fog. I never spoke of it to anybody. I didn't want to hear the ridicule from family and friends who knew me . . . and knew that I could never achieve dreams of this magnitude.

And just in a snap of the fingers, just like the little boy under the maple tree in my childhood backyard, I would be transported back into the "real" world. I wasn't sure what was fantasy and what was real. *What is the truth about my identity and destiny?* was the shadowy question that haunted me.

I had many conversations throughout my life that would illuminate my next steps in my Quest to discover and achieve my Dream. In these moments of honest vulnerability, I would reveal small bits of the Dream to others to get their feedback. It was humbling to hear how others saw me. I ran into many others who were on their very own Dreamer's Quests.

When I was in high school, I was one of several youth interns at church. The other interns and I were on an overnight with the junior high group. It was our responsibility to keep an eye on the campers through the night—we called it "rat patrol." However, we talked into the early morning hours about what God might have in mind for our futures. It was transformative to Dream together.

Then much later there were the conversations when I was a youth pastor with one of my volunteers named Randy. He was a total radical and was a true product of the late '60s/early '70s Jesus Movement. His fervor for following God inspired me. We encouraged each other and enjoyed our conversations together.

We had a conversation standing in the church parking lot one summer afternoon. We both had other places to be, but it was like we *had* to be together to share something important. I shared, for the first time with anybody outside my family, that I thought God had something big in mind for my life. He came right back with, "Me too! I thought I was the only one!"

I was embarrassed to tell Randy that I had been to the entrance of the Dream Gate on several occasions before. Each time, I would peer through the doors into the Land of my Dream, but I never stepped through the gate. On several occasions I had inched my way a little deeper in and stayed on the main path to a crossroad. I knew it was a point of decision and commitment. But I would make a quick retreat to the safety of the other side of the gate, back in the land of Ordinary.

However, the longing in my soul would cause me to investigate this land again and again. I became at home just inside the gate, seeing a bit more clearly the path that God had designed for me, but not clearly enough to really come alive in my soul. My spirit longed for more, but my mind said no: *Too much risk and danger lie this way. Stay here: just inside the gate is far enough.*

Sometimes I would inch my way down the path, only to stop at the first crossroad. I would make sure I never lost view of the gate that opened back into Ordinary, where I could always retreat to my familiar, safe life among the Dreamless.

It was at the entrance of the Dream gate that I would spend many days trying to convince myself that I had, in fact, followed my Dream. But that was a lie. Deep down inside I knew it wasn't true. Meanwhile, the longing of my soul sounded an alarm I couldn't shut off. I was half alive and half dead. I was awake, and yet, I was still asleep.

The struggle and pain were real, but that's about all that was real in that life of compromise. I thought that if I could just ride out this pain in my soul, eventually I would get over it and be able to understand my Dream—my destiny. I tried to numb the pain (my go-to pain killers were eating, sleeping, and entertainment with a side of lots of people and activity), only to find that it took ever-increasing doses of numbing agents. But numbing my pain had the nasty side effect of clouding my Dream. The more I numbed my pain, the less I could see my vision for my future.

* * *

If I asked you who held the most successful evangelist campaign—in any city in the world, of all time—who would you say?

Billy Graham, D L Moody, Billy Sunday, The Apostle Paul?

How about Jonah? Would he make your Top Ten List of all-time great evangelists?

Ancient Nineveh was an Assyrian city in Upper Mesopotamia (around modern-day northern Iraq). It was located on the eastern bank of the Tigris River, and it was the capital city of Assyrian Empire at one time. It held the status of being the largest city in the world for about fifty years, until 612 BC. Scholars estimate the population at or just above 120 thousand, making it ten to one hundred times larger than most villages of that time. It was not only large in population, but also in physical size. It would have taken three days to travel across the breadth of the city during the time of Jonah.

After receiving his Awakening—when God called him to preach to Nineveh—Jonah took a couple of detours. (We will talk about them a bit later.) After these detours, when Jonah finally made his way into the city, it took him three days to preach his message to whole city. The response was total repentance of the entire city. That repentance reached all the way to the king, who decreed that everybody was to worship God and repent. Every living being in Nineveh—all 120,000, plus every living animal—was to repent, put on sackcloth, and worship God.

How's that for an evangelistic campaign? Jonah had game! Or was it that God had designed him for this task? That God had placed him at this time in history? That God had written him into the history books before the foundation of the world—to be the right person with the right message for such a time as this?

Is this what Jonah is known for? No, we know him as the guy that got swallowed by a big fish. How did he get himself into the belly of a fish? How did he live through the ordeal? What can we learn from his detours of denial, disobedience and pain?

The opening lines of the book of Jonah tell us who the author of this script really is: God.

> *The word of the LORD came to Jonah son of Amittai: "Go to the great city of Nineveh and preach against it, because its wickedness has come up before me."*

Jonah 1:1, 2

Notice that we find the Psalms 139 formula for a Dream. God clicked Jonah's DNA into place ("son of Amittai"). God wrote the script ("The word of the Lord came to Jonah"). God had a mission for Jonah. He had written him into the annals of history before Adam and Eve took their first breath. God had created Jonah just the way He wanted him to be for this role.

Look again at verses 1 and 2. It doesn't say: "The word of the Lord came to Jonah: 'Go get on a ship. Get yourself thrown overboard during a terrible storm. I'll make sure you are swallowed by an enormous fish, and the fish will throw you up on a beach three days later.'"

No, God had already declared Jonah's Dream, the mission he was to embark upon. It was Jonah's choice to head in the opposite direction—a path that included storms, rejection, and the despair of living three days in circumstances that resembled death. It was after his prayer of confession and worship that God had him puked up on a beach, and Jonah Awakened again to God's purpose for his life.

I'm sure Jonah didn't think too long about getting back on the path of The Dreamer's Quest. Crawling up onto the beach (covered in slime, I imagine) he had the choice: to follow the Dream that God had for him, or to go through the ringer for another round.

Jonah decided to go and preach to the city. But he really didn't want to. He wanted God to destroy the city, not to forgive its inhabitants. So, in his anger towards God and the city, he tweaked the message and preached that destruction was coming to Nineveh. God used Jonah's preaching to cause repentance.

Next, we find Jonah sitting up on a hill to await God's verdict. He was angry—he had decided that judgment was what Nineveh deservers, not mercy. At the close of this story, we find a bitter prophet sitting on a hill, gazing at the greatest repentance of any city in history, and not being able to come to terms not only with God sparing the city, but with God creating him to be the messenger.

It is tragic to be designed for such an important mission and almost miss it—almost miss it because you fight against the script He has written for you. The account of Nineveh's repentance can be found not only in the Bible, but also in the Jewish Tanakh and in the Muslim Koran. Jonah's story has been told worldwide, and its message is timeless. That's partly because of the repentance of Nineveh, but mostly we know this story because of Jonah's rejection of God's call.

Jonah had become content with Ordinary. He did not want to be part of Extraordinary. We do not know if it was prejudice against the Ninevites, or a wrong committed by them against Jonah or his family, or a strong sense of moral righteousness—that they deserved punishment. God is a God of mercy, grace, and compassion (Jonah 4:1-3). Whatever the personal issue was, Jonah's story ends with anger toward God, bitterness, and an ungrateful spirit about his design and story.

Jonah's story sits in sharp contrast to the story of Joseph. Jonah viewed himself as a victim rather than a victor. It was a much different story with Joseph.

After his brothers captured Joseph, they tied him up and threw him down a well to teach him a lesson. *Look who's bowing now.* Going too far in their plot, they sold Joseph into slavery. He was taken to Egypt where he was sold to a high-ranking official as a household slave.

Joseph kept his Dream alive. He worked harder and was smarter than any of the other slaves in the official's household. He knew he was supposed to be a leader, so he acted like one. He kept the Dream alive by continuing along in the Dreamer's Quest. He was not overcome by what looked like impossible circumstances. He kept growing and learning. Soon, he was put in charge of the entire household. Joseph had quickly become responsible for the personal affairs of this rich ruler (while remaining a slave).

The Dreamer's Quest can take its twists and turns, landing you in some very low places. But the journey is designed to ready you for your Dream. All you must do is stay on course. God will see you through it.

* * *

I made the decision to go to Cornerstone University (formerly known as Grand Rapids Baptist College). Three very different reasons drove my decision.

- When I was with the guys that I played sports with, I would say the reason was to play on the sports teams. I knew I could walk on to the baseball and cross-country teams, and I was pretty sure I could win a spot on the basketball team.

- When I was talking with my parents, pastors, teachers, and people at church, I would say I was going there to become a youth pastor.

- When I was alone with my thoughts, I would tell myself that I would go seeking a good time. Maybe I would find something fun to do for the rest of my life. But that's not important now. Having a good time is what is important now.

Before long, I was engrossed in so many activities and classes that I had little time for fun. I made all three sports teams and carried a full load of classes. I began classes at 7:45 a.m. on Mondays, Wednesdays, and Fridays, and at 8:00 a.m. on Tuesdays and Thursdays, with a quick lunch between morning and afternoon classes. Then it was off to cross-country practice at 3:15 p.m., finishing practice around 5:30 p.m. I would eat dinner on the run, and then it was back to the gym for pre-season basketball workouts. I would finish around 8:30 p.m. Then I'd shower, study for a few minutes, and do it all again the next day. After cross-country finished, it was down to one sport in the winter (basketball) and one sport in the spring (baseball).

Each team scheduled games all over the Midwest: mainly in Michigan and Indiana, with a couple trips to Ohio and the Chicago area. My freshman year, just for fun, I also traveled with the college band some weekends to perform in churches (I played the saxophone).

After working at General Motors the summer between my freshman and sophomore years, I was not ready to start the grind again. The thought had been in the back of my mind for months that I was missing out on a lot of fun. On the drive back to college, I decided: I was going "all in for fun," whatever that meant.

I began to hatch a plan. I would have to change my major, because preparing to be a youth pastor would cramp my style. And my girlfriend would have to go. She would never go for this change of heart and direction. I would have to break up with her soon. Why not as soon as I got back on campus? Done!

I walked into the cafeteria, looked around, found my girlfriend and said, "This is not working out. We are going to have to break up." I wouldn't answer any of her questions about why; I just walked off. Man, how cold can you get? I don't think she ever understood it was my rebellion against God that caused the break-up. It had nothing to do with her. She was a godly girl who would not approve of my rebellion against God's plan for my life. I still feel regret about the plan I cooked up to add some "fun" into my life.

Like the prodigal son, I wasted a year and a half of my life. I found a new girlfriend that I thought was "the one" for me. She ended up engaged to another guy about three weeks after she broke up with me. I thought I had found real friends, who suddenly left school in the middle of the semester. (I have never heard from them since. I do not even know how to contact them.) I burned bridges with two sports I loved—cross-country and basketball—and fell well below my potential in baseball, the sport I was most talented in. I almost lost my life to drugs and alcohol. I lost the respect of my closest friends. It was bad—really bad.

After hitting rock bottom, I sat in a rocking chair in my apartment for three days and reflected on the mess I had created. It occurred to me: *Maybe God is trying to get my attention.* Duh! I was kind of like Jonah in the belly of the fish, realizing that God was very serious about him preaching to Nineveh! How dumb could I have been? (Don't answer that.)

It was then I got a phone call from a professor's assistant to set up an appointment as soon as possible. It was not a request, but rather a demand, that I be there. Almost as soon as I had hung up the phone, an assistant for *another* professor called to set up an appointment with me an hour after the other appointment.

Oh man, was I in trouble. I didn't know what they had on me, but it could be any number of violations of the code of conduct. I guessed this was my answer from God.

I had made an all-in commitment to pursue the Dream He had implanted within. Now that I was all-in on God's plan, it looked like God was pulling the plug on my Dream. Now what?

To my surprise, the meetings weren't about things I had done, but things I had *not* done. It was not a pleasant afternoon. The professors scheduled back-to-back meetings, each taking his turn at tough love. They confronted me about my lack of commitment to the program and the call of God on my life. There was also a heavy dose of statements like, "I see great potential in you, and you are wasting it!" Dr. Ron Chadwick and Dr. Dan Stevens kicked my butt that day. It was just what I needed.

I went to work right away. I was not sure I could salvage my education and my career as a youth pastor, but I was all in – I began to say that I was "Totally (all in) and radically (recklessly abandoned) committed to the cause of Christ." My life began to make sense again. I could see clearly that God had a plan, and that I had a starring role in it.

I later realized that I had moved beyond the crossroads near the entrance of the Gate, and I was on a new path leading to a new place I had never been before. In the land of Vision. I had moved down the path toward the overlook, where I would see the lands I'd journey to in the future. More and more of the Dream that God had planted within my soul was making its way from my heart to my head.

For the first time, I wrote down spectacular goals for my life. I had no idea how or when they would ever come true, but I knew one day I would somehow achieve them. My next stop would be at the overlook, where I would discover exactly what I was committing to achieve.

* * *

THE DREAMER'S JOURNAL

Ron Wayne was one of the founders of the second-most valuable company in the world today. Apple founders Steve Jobs, Steve Wozniak, and Ron Wayne incorporated Apple Computers on April 2, 1976. They had a dream to create the world's best personal computer, which was a new sector during the age of the mainframe computer.

However, twelve days later, Ron Wayne had second thoughts. He didn't see how he fit into the Dream and how he could contribute to the company with giants like Jobs and Wozniak. He decided to sell his 10 percent share of the company back to the other partners for $800.

As of today, his 10 percent stake in the company would be worth about $14.63 *billion!* That would place him among the richest men in the world. However, ever since that decision, he has had a lifetime of financial struggles. Recently he sold off his original paperwork from the company to collectors for about $40,000 to pay his bills.

While one can only wonder about what really happened behind the scenes during the first twelve days of the Apple story, Ron's story teaches us that there is a cost to losing sight of your Dream. Imagine what the consequences of not achieving it might be—not only for yourself, but also for your family and the world.

The world is waiting for you to step into your Dream! We need your contribution!

3

ACTIVATING YOUR DREAM! THE CALLING OF TOTAL AND RADICAL COMMITMENT

You always have two choices: your commitment versus your fear.

Sammy Davis, Jr.

* * *

We use the same plot for many of the stories we tell. The hero is living an ordinary life in an ordinary time and place. But, unknown to them, they are anything but ordinary, and the time and place is also anything but ordinary. Our hero has a call to adventure. The hero refuses, until they meet a mentor. They come to a crossing into a new world. There are tests, allies, and enemies. The hero must face his inner self. Then the hero faces the ordeal and wins the reward. The hero returns to Ordinary a changed person. We tell the same tales repeatedly. We change the names, places, and times, but we use the same structure of the story each time.

I believe the reason we use this structure is because it is the story of all of us. We all think we are ordinary people living ordinary lives. What we don't realize is that we are anything but ordinary, and our lives are scripted by the master storyteller—our Creator. There is a story residing within each and every one of us. It is when we awaken to this universal story that we begin to discover our personal story.

For me, it has happened on several occasions. Like the time when I was a young boy of nine years, sitting in church on New Year's Eve of 1970, listening to my oldest brother preach. I had never heard him preach before, and the sermon made a huge impression on me. His sermon was "Make Sure Your Salvation."

For the first time, I knew I needed to make sure I had a personal relationship with the Creator. Even though I had prayed many times and I had been baptized, I needed to make sure. So that night about 1:00 a.m. on January 1, 1970, after coming home from the all-night church service, I did just that. It was a commitment to follow Jesus no matter what. In those early morning hours, I had my first thoughts of being a pastor to teens.

Another time was when I made the same type of commitment after three days in a rocking chair, trying to figure out my life. I made the commitment to follow God no matter what the cost. I knew God was going to use me for something big. What the big thing was going to be I didn't know, but I knew it was going to happen. The first of many "big things" happened about three months later when I was elected Student Body President of the college.

Later after being a youth pastor for nearly ten years, when I was speaking with Randy, the radical. I let it slip out that I believe God was going to do something big with my life: that I felt called to speak to teens. I could imagine standing before a couple thousand young people speaking. That happened about a year later, at a national youth gathering of a couple thousand people.

I had another awakening when I attended a conference for youth pastors from around the world. We had a prayer meeting with about fifty youth leaders in attendance. I recommitted to live a life of following Jesus, wherever He might take me. I felt God preparing me to participate in a prayer movement that would lead to a renewal of commitment to follow Jesus. That happened about five years later, with a group of youth pastors meeting together twice a month—praying for revival.

Then there are the housing stories—where God provided a place for our family to live over thirty-six years. Or the money stories—where God provided just enough money to carry us through a time of need. Each time, we had no idea where the money was going to come from. Or the ministry stories—where God put us in the right place at the right time to achieve something very special. On and on, the stories keep coming.

Clarity comes with an Awakening! An Awakening must happen for you to see the Dreamer's Quest. To have an Awakening, you must first see yourself in the eyes of the Creator—that you are a masterpiece with a purpose. That you have been placed in the right place at the right time to achieve the purpose the Creator has designed you for. The Awakening is when you see the truth about *who* you are, *what* you are designed for, *where* you are going, and *how* you are going to get there. These all come together to describe your *why* in life.

* * *

Daniel, who faced a den of lions overnight, has a very similar story to Joseph's. If we place them side-by-side, we see how God guides us *through* hard times, not *out* of hard times. In fact, your commitment to your calling will take you directly through hard times.

Hard times had come to Daniel and his companions. The last two tribes of Israel, Benjamin and Judah, had fallen into the hands of King Nebuchadnezzar, King of Babylon. Not only did Nebuchadnezzar conquer Judah and Benjamin, he took the gold and silver objects of worship from the temple back to Babylon as spoils of war. To finalize his campaign to rule over all Israel, he captured the leading young people of Israel. He took them back to Babylon for indoctrination training, designed to gain loyalty and control over his captives.

It was Nebuchadnezzar's custom to place his young trainees in positions of leadership after they had been indoctrinated and their allegiance had been turned toward him. Among these captives from Judah we find four young men who are Awakening to their own Dreamer's Quests: Daniel, Shadrach, Meshach, and Abednego.

They had witnessed the destruction of the temple, of their government, and of those who stood against Babylon and King Nebuchadnezzar. They knew what was expected of them—to conform to the Babylonian way of life and to bow to the sovereignty of their new king. They also knew that if they did not excel above the others, they would be eliminated by execution. Just a *little* bit of pressure and stress was placed on these four young men.

Daniel, like Joseph, was now a slave. In Daniel 1:8, we pick up his story to find that he had been taken into captivity and placed in the King's retraining program in Babylon. However, Daniel had resolved not to defile himself with the Babylonian customs. His first test came when he was faced with a diet that violated God's law. He was determined not to compromise his beliefs by following the King's diet, but to follow the diet provided within Jewish law.

Daniel's resolve is to find a way to remain faithful to his commitment to God. We are told that Daniel went to the man in charge of the training program with a proposal to test the Jewish diet against the King's diet. Daniel was more concerned with his relationship with God than the king. And he was willing to put that relationship to the test.

What faith! Would you have so much certainty to follow God's plan that you would put your life at risk? This is the type of faith that God rewards. This is the type of faith that will move mountains. God not only rewarded Daniel's faith, but he also blessed him and his three companions with health, wisdom, and strength above and beyond the other captives'.

Many years before Daniel's dietary challenge, Joseph found himself in a similar situation that could have compromised him. We find Joseph was now a slave in Egypt to a man named Potiphar. Joseph's circumstances also required devotion to God. Because of his commitment to work with excellence, God blessed him and Potiphar. Joseph began moving up the ranks within the household. Potiphar placed everything within his home under Joseph's care and control. When he did this, God blessed everything within his house and field.

Potiphar was able to turn over everything to Joseph, concerning himself with only the food he ate. Talk about hiring the right guy! Potiphar's success probably made him seem smart to other high-ranking officials in Egypt. But his wife took note of Joseph. She began to plot an affair between Joseph and herself.

However, Joseph refused her advances. He explained to her that Potiphar had given him complete control of everything within his household. Joseph had access to everything that Potiphar owned except his wife. Then he said something very interesting: "How, then, could I do such a wicked thing and sin against God?"

Joseph took decisive action—he escaped from her immediately. As he ran, Potiphar's wife grabbed his coat and held it in her hands until her husband came home. She lied and turned the story against Joseph, saying that he had made unwanted advances toward her. This landed Joseph in prison.

Sometimes the path you must take may look like it will cause you great harm. However, this path is the correct one for your Dreamer's Quest, even though it will cost you everything you have. God is guiding you into the Dream he has designed you for. It is through hardships that you will discover your path to greatness. Your commitment to follow the path designed for you will lead you closer to the Dream designed for you.

* * *

Like I mentioned before, my Dreamer's Quest has been the adventure of a lifetime! It had its Awakening in my childhood and many re-Awakenings throughout my life. You would think that if you become alive to your passion, you would stick with it. However, there are sacrifices and battles that lie in your path that can derail you from the Quest. We will look at some of them later in the book—but, for now, it is enough to know that you may be at your first grand Awakening. Either way, this is the crossroad in the land of the Dream that every traveler must come to: Am I all in? Am I totally and radically committed to this journey?

For me, clarity has come at moments of deep commitment to the Creator's design as I travel the path of the Dreamer's Quest. Each time I made that commitment, I had a moment of great clarity. I could see my destination with great detail. I had a vision for the future. I could see it, hear it, taste it, smell it, and feel it. The details of my destination became crystal clear. Most of the time I could not tell you exactly how I was going to reach my Dream, other than to say, "God has it under control."

This is where your faith comes into play. You know you must go to the place that has been revealed within your soul, but you have no idea how to get there. You only trust that the Creator has designed you for this purpose and has placed you within this story to succeed.

Your sight is not in the physical world, where you can examine the details of the destination. It is written upon your heart, within your soul. Sometimes you are the only one who can see it clearly. It is as real to you as looking out your window in the morning.

Hebrews 11:1-3
11 Now faith is confidence in what we hope for and assurance about what we do not see. ² This is what the ancients were commended for.

³ By faith we understand that the universe was formed at God's command, so that what is seen was not made out of what was visible.

Just seeing it is not enough. You now must act upon what God has given you. You must both see and commit to the Quest to take hold of what the Creator has called you to do. You embark on the Quest with faith that it is up to the Creator to prepare you for the Quest and to make sure of your success.

Hebrews 11:6
⁶ And without faith it is impossible to please God, because anyone who comes to him must believe that he exists and that he rewards those who earnestly seek him.

It is impossible to embark on The Dreamer's Quest without a deep faith in the Creator—faith that He is not only your creator and savior, but that He is the author and perfecter of your faith. That He knows who you are, He knows the Dream He has entrusted to you, and He is going to guide you to achieve that Dream.

Hebrews 12:1-3
12 Therefore, since we are surrounded by such a great cloud of witnesses, let us throw off everything that hinders

and the sin that so easily entangles. And let us run with perseverance the race marked out for us, ² fixing our eyes on Jesus, the pioneer and perfecter of faith. For the joy set before him he endured the cross, scorning its shame, and sat down at the right hand of the throne of God. ³ Consider him who endured such opposition from sinners, so that you will not grow weary and lose heart.

Faith is the fuel that drives this deep commitment. Our total and radical commitment allows the illumination of the Creator to light the way to the Dream written upon our souls. This is the Awakening, which leads to the Dreamer's Quest.

Faith is the total and radical commitment to the plan that the Creator has for your life, a humbling of yourself, giving in to the Creator's plan and not your own, that will ignite your soul with a fire of passion.

Conversely, it is the rejection of the Creator's design that will cloud your Dream, leaving a soul that is in pain, numb or asleep. The choice is yours: awakened and alive, or asleep and dead.

The all-in attitude required to set out on the Quest is more than some can endure. But until you begin you cannot reach your goal. As the saying goes, "There are no mountains for climbers."

I gained clarity of vision as I made the commitment to be exactly who the Creator had designed me to be. Taking the clues from my childhood, embracing the Dream placed within my soul, I began to see beyond the present and into the future: my true identity and what I should be doing.

The draw I felt to be a professional athlete was not a call to be great at a sport, but to be part of a team that worked together for a common cause. To become a member of a tribe of visionaries who supported each other on their Dreamer's Quests.

My passion to be a forest ranger had little to do with the national park system, and much more to do with the visionaries who saw the beauty of the Creator's work and wanted to preserve those creations unmarred by destructive behaviors. I saw their passion to maintain the original design of the creation. I saw their willingness to run into a forest fire to protect the creation. Both passions were just signposts for a deeper passion to help individuals protect their personal, God-given design. Like a park ranger who provides a protective environment so the creation can thrive, I am called to maintain a space for my tribe.

My desire to be an air traffic controller has found its way into my journey as I assist others to arrive at their intended destinations. I guide those who need vision to achieve their Dream while pursuing their Dreamer's Quests.

My gifts to be a teacher have not only been used in educational institutions, but also in the area of speaking. God has designed me to share my experiences and to guide others through places I have been before.

* * *

THE DREAMER'S JOURNAL

Abraham Lincoln was the right person, living in the right time and place, to rise to the occasion to lead his nation. He saw not only what he needed to do, but also what the nation needed to do. This was in a time of great confusion, divisiveness, and destruction. Yet, with a homespun education and humor, Lincoln secured election after declaring his message of a United States without slavery. He was totally and radically committed to this Dream.

However, he did not bring a long list of successful achievements with him to the Presidential race of 1860. Here are some of the failures of Abraham Lincoln, sprinkled with a couple of his successes:

- 1831: Lost his job
- 1832: Defeated for Illinois State Legislature
- 1833: Failed in business
- 1834: Elected to Illinois State Legislature (success)
- 1835: Sweetheart died
- 1836: Had nervous breakdown
- 1838: Defeated for Illinois House Speaker
- 1843: Defeated for nomination for U.S. Congress
- 1846: Elected to Congress (success)
- 1848: Lost re-nomination
- 1849: Rejected for land officer position
- 1854: Defeated for U.S. Senate seat
- 1856: Defeated for nomination for Vice President
- 1858: Defeated for U.S. Senate a second time
- 1860: Elected President (success)

Yet his Dreamer's Quest placed him in the White House during the gravest moments in U.S. history.

PART 2

To Believe—Acquiring!

Tripp has committed himself to embark upon the Dreamer's Quest. He is determined to complete this journey. Although there are moments that he doubts his decision, he determines to stay another night. As he has made his way through the land of Dream, he has left Ordinary behind. Even though he has made an all-in commitment to the Quest, he has much to learn. While excited for what lies ahead, he also senses a need to understand more about the journey that awaits him.

While he explores this land, he catches glimpses of another gate. Tripp's uncertainty and indecision have been his greatest obstacles up to this point in his journey. He stops at the sight of the gate and hopes this gateway will reveal more information about the Quest ahead. The path that he has chosen seems to lead toward this new gate. Tripp feels both excited and tentative as he draws closer to the new gate. Will he gain the information he needs to continue the Dreamer's Quest?

Taking the path he thinks will lead him to the gate, he hears the unmistakable sound of a horse in a canter approaching from behind. He peers over his shoulder to see a fellow traveler atop a white stallion. He is excited to see it is the same Traveler who encouraged him to enter the land of Dream. At the speed she is going, she will pass by him rather quickly. Tripp waves her down. As she slows her horse's pace to a slow walk, she looks down and says, "I see you made it this far. Have you found your answers?" Tripp notices the same look of determination and purpose she had in her eyes before. But this time, he also sees a look of care and compassion for him.

"I have a much clearer perspective about my design and my story," Tripp answered. "I have also made an oath to complete the Dreamer's Quest. But I feel I have so much to learn. Where am I going to get the details—the missing pieces—that I need to complete my Quest?"

"You are headed in the right direction. Have you seen the gate ahead?" the Traveler inquires.

"Yes, I have caught a couple of quick glimpses of it. Is this the right way?" Tripp responds.

"Yes, you will be there before nightfall. I have responsibilities in the land beyond the Believe Gate this afternoon. I will see you there soon. But make sure you look me up at the entrance of the gate beyond this one. It's very different from the first two gates. I will accompany you through the land beyond that gate. It's always good to have a fellow traveler when you face impediments."

That last statement causes Tripp to consider the weight of her words. *I want a guide, but what will be so different about this land that I will need one?* he wonders. The conflicting thoughts cause a bit of concern and fear. *What have I got myself into now?* he begins to shout within his mind. He reminds himself of his oath to complete the Dreamer's Quest. He resolves to keep moving forward one step at a time.

"Before you need to worry about that land, you have some work ahead of you. Travel this path to the next gate. Soak in as much as you can in the next land before you attempt to pass through the third gate. I will meet you there. Godspeed!" And with that, she is off in a gallop down the path. As she makes the turn, she once again looks over her shoulder at Tripp and smiles. Pointing with two fingers, the rider shows the way and then she disappears around the bend.

As Tripp makes the turn the Traveler disappeared around, he begins to clearly see the gate. It looks like an Ivy League University. However, rather than being boring, Tripp gets the feeling that that the gate holds exciting revelations for him, and for any who would come this way. The gate has the word *Believe* placed above the entrance. As he gets closer, Tripp reads aloud the inscription on the door: "To Observe with Competence."

His view beyond the gate is of a land filled with several large buildings, made of stone and ancient timber. For those who pass through the Believe Gate, they soon discover a wealth of knowledge stored within the huge structures fashioned from fieldstones by expert builders. Travelers who have made the Quest before speak about the various gates, and about what travelers might encounter upon their journeys. Tripp makes his way into the first of many buildings. The furnishings within these buildings are strong and sturdy—much like the travelers who speak within them. There he finds other travelers engaged in the study of new knowledge to guide them upon their journeys.

Tripp soon discovers, as he studies the words of the Original Designer and other Travelers, that his task here in Believe is to acquire the standards given by the Creator. He also discovers that the information revealed here will guide him upon his Quest.

One bright afternoon, Tripp notices a large crowd gathering at the entrance of a lecture hall. To Tripp's surprise, the speaker is the Traveler who gave directions to him back in Ordinary and in the land of Dream. Tripp is amazed to hear the Traveler share her experiences of adventure and mishaps. But what really impresses Tripp is the solid foundation of belief that the Traveler has. Her acquisition of ethics, values, standards, and worldview have become the foundational building blocks to her beliefs. By obtaining this foundation, she has developed the character needed to pass the tests she has faced on her many journeys. Tripp attempts to get the Traveler's attention, but as soon as she finishes sharing, she slips away through a gate Tripp knows he will have to enter one day—maybe one day soon.

For now, Tripp places his focus on gathering and understanding as much information about the Quest as he can. Most of the lessons that Tripp hears in his extended stay in this land center upon three main themes: Faith, Hope and Love. While Tripp's interaction with other travelers is limited because he had not completed his journey to several of the gates, he always finds them to be very encouraging. He enjoyed sharing a meal with a traveler, listening to the lectures, and studying the vast library that houses the adventures and memoirs of thousands of travelers who have gone before him.

Tripp often thinks about the Traveler who encouraged and guided him to begin his Quest. He really doesn't know much about her, but he still has a deep affinity towards her. He follows her advice to drink deep from the fountains of learning in this land.

Tripp notices that, even though he was eager to continue with his Quest, his extended stay in this land has been very valuable to him personally. His new understanding of the Quest and the training has transformed him deeply. His desire for personal enrichment to find his meaning in life begins to give way to a new purpose—to serve others. Tripp begins to have a burden for the family and friends he left behind in Ordinary. He gains great satisfaction in assisting those who enter the Believe Gate for the first time. This passion has been passed along by his mentors, who have shared stories of their battles.

Tripp ponders what may await him in the next land. But for now, he enjoys this land of refreshment of mind and soul, while bracing himself for the struggles that await him.

4

OBSERVING YOUR MIND:
THE NEW PRINCIPLES
DESIGNED FOR THE QUEST

Three things are necessary for the salvation of man: to know what he ought to believe; to know what he ought to desire; and to know what he ought to do.

Thomas Aquinas

* * *

I t has happened to me so many times before! I make a total and radical commitment to the Dreamer's Quest! I take a few steps to move toward my Dream. Then it seems like the Creator goes silent. As soon as I say I'm all in, there comes a moment of silence. I become frustrated and second-guess my commitment.

I would plead with God, "Are you there? I'm all-in. I said I would do anything you want me to do. Send me a sign! I'm listening . . . I will wait for you . . . please, show me what to do now!"

Then, silence.

47

In the past, at the first sign of difficulty I would demand that God remove me from the trials I faced. Like the little boy sitting under the maple tree in the backyard, I'd revert to another round of dialogues with God—this time, instead of negotiations, they'd be more complaints. Making sure to list the risks I had taken, I would demand that God act to relieve me of the stress of my situation. It is easy to lose all hope in these moments of distress.

I took my biggest risk of my life in 2008. We left a great ministry to start a new one in Orlando. I felt that God was leading me to create something new and different. I moved my family to Orlando, Florida without a safety net. Armed only with the Dream that had haunted me for years and few supporters who had seen something in our hearts that called them to partner with us, we made the leap of faith into the unknown.

Our plan was to build a ministry from the ground up. There was no church or ministry asking us to move and serve there. There was no job waiting to pay the bills. There was no network to plug into. Just my relationship with the Creator and my belief that He wanted me to do this.

I took along with me on my Quest my wife and my five daughters, who ranged in ages from fifteen to twenty-two years old. Not only was I all in with *my* life, but also the lives of six others who I loved.

The first few weeks of our move were intense! We moved into our new home in Winter Garden, Florida on September 11, 2008. Little did I know that 1,100 miles north, in New York city, the Federal Reserve Chairman Timothy Geithner, Treasury Secretary Henry Paulson, and others would meet at the Fed the very next day to discuss the fate of Lehman Brothers. The Lehman Brothers bankruptcy sparked a series of events on Wall Street that shocked all of us. The "too big to fail" AIG bailout, TARP, the government acquisition of nine U.S. banks, and the bailout for General Motors, Chrysler, and Bank of America all had profound effect on each of us in the United States.

These events also had a very intense impact on our ministry plans. I had taken a leap of faith, and the ground had moved from under me. Before I could make a clean landing, all my plans no longer made sense. I was left falling, with my wife and five daughters in tow.

I was not too big to fail! There would be no bailouts for me. There would only be phone calls from supporters who could no longer keep their commitments to give like they had hoped to. Overnight, stock values and retirement plans were being wiped out. Nobody was able to obtain loans. Every day, businesses were being closed. Our start-up ministry was in crisis, but our cries for help were drowned out by the cries of the nation.

I began to take walks in the unfinished residential development behind our house. We had rented a house on the edge of the work stoppage. The banking and housing crises had halted all work within the community. There were miles of roads built ready for new houses with all the infrastructure in place, including the lamp posts. We began to call the empty neighborhood behind us "Narnia" because of the lamp posts that lined the streets. It was an eerie feeling, walking alone in this land of unbuilt dreams.

But it was a perfect place for me to walk and to lay out my complaints against God. I was in a desperate situation. I did not know how I would feed and house my family; let alone how I would ever move forward with my Dream. I had put all kinds of plans together that would cost thousands of dollars, and I didn't even have enough money to pay for rent and food.

As I walked in "Narnia," I would pray to God—okay, I would *rant* to God about this situation I found myself in. "Why did you bring me to Orlando to destroy me?" was the theme of my rants. I couldn't let go of how good I had it back in Columbus, Ohio. Why in the world did I ever leave there? I was better off half-alive there than dead on arrival here in Florida.

My faith was broken, and I had lost hope. I was in a crisis. Could I ever get out of this downward spiral of despair? The loss of hope had become greater than my faith. I was sinking fast.

* * *

You've got to love Peter! He is bold. He has faith. He says stupid stuff. He does stupid stuff. He is so human. If God can use Peter, He can use us as well.

The story about Peter walking on water is found only in the book of Matthew (Matt. 14:22-33). The gospels of Mark and John only tell about Jesus walking on water, and Luke leaves the entire story out. It is only the book of Matthew includes the exchange between Peter and Jesus that led to Peter's walk of faith.

Jesus had just fed more than 5,000 people using only a little boy's lunch of five loaves and two fish. Not only did this feed the entire crowd, but the disciples had also taken up twelve baskets of leftovers. This was not their first rodeo. They had watched as Jesus had taught the people, fed the hungry, calmed the storm, healed the sick, freed the demon-possessed, and raised the dead.

After a long day of teaching, miracles, and serving people's needs, Jesus told the disciples to cross to the other side of The Sea of Galilee. He said he would join them later. Not questioning how He would join them, they entered a fishing boat and began to make the crossing. The Sea of Galilee was a large body of water about 8 miles across east to west and 13 miles north to south, with an average depth of 84 feet.

Jesus went up on a hillside, possibly atop the natural amphitheater He had used to address the crowd earlier that day. From this vantage point, He would have had a view of the entire Sea of Galilee. We are told that He watched over the disciples while he spent the night in prayer. His followers encountered a storm, and they were not able to make the crossing because of the waves and wind.

Early in the morning hours, Jesus decided it was time for Him to make the crossing. So, in God-like fashion, Jesus walked . . . across the top of the water. When the disciples saw Jesus walk by, they were terrified. Jesus called out to them and told them not to fear—it was just Him, Jesus.

The story takes an interesting twist here. Peter had been admiring the way Jesus was able to walk with ease across the top of the waves. (It probably looked a lot easier than rowing the boat against the wind.) With a measure of faith, but in the spirit of a TSA agent checking ID at the airport, Peter called out to Jesus, "Lord, if it's you, tell me to come to you on the water." (I'm not sure what Peter would have done if a voice came back with, "No, it's Bill.")

Jesus directly answered both questions posed by Peter with a one-word response, "Come."

We are not told the look on Peter's face. Neither are we told his response time, nor what he was thinking. We are only told that he got out of the boat and walked on the water, heading for Jesus. Wow! Nobody else can claim that they got of a boat and walked on water. Just Peter and Jesus, as far as I know.

But something happened during this short walk. Really, four things happened:

1. He saw his circumstance rather than his savior—Peter looked around and saw the waves.

2. He became afraid—the sight of the waves caused fear within Peter.

3. He began to sink—the miracle had come to an abrupt conclusion.

4. He cried out, "Lord save me!"—Then came phase two of this miracle: Jesus walking on water while supporting the weight of Peter, too.

We are told that, immediately, Jesus reached out his hand and caught Peter before he went under (Maybe Jesus let him bob for a moment or two, but the word "immediately" tells us He was there before Peter went under).

Then we get to sit in on a moment of restoration between Jesus and his very wet disciple, Peter. Jesus asked Peter:

"You of little faith," he said, "why did you doubt?"

Matthew 14:31b

The first new rule to this land of Believe is that you must observe what you think about. You need to screen the input into your mind, and discipline yourself to stay focused on the clarity already given to you. Isaiah 26:3 says this:

You will keep in perfect peace those whose minds are steadfast, because they trust in you.

Isaiah 26:3

V. Raymond Edman, the fourth president of Wheaton College, has been credited with saying, "Never doubt in the darkness what God gave you in the light." To really believe, you must act. You must get out of the boat. But once out of the boat, you may encounter waves. It is then that your faith will be put to the test. By staying focused on God, you will keep the clarity and peace you received before. These moments will strengthen your lack of faith to continue.

Who among you fears the LORD
and obeys the word of his servant?
Let the one who walks in the dark,

who has no light,
trust in the name of the LORD
and rely on their God.

Isaiah 50:11

If Peter had kept his mind focused only Jesus and His invitation to "Come," he would have made the short walk without incident. However, just like most of us do from time to time, he took his attention off Jesus. And, just like Peter, we often focus on the darkness that surrounds us, the waves that threaten us, and the other distractions that take us off-course from our Dream.

To Observe with Competence is the ability to exercise faith, to rely on the truth, and to focus on what God has called us to do. However, sometimes we let our minds get entangled in the affairs of this world, and we lose perspective. We need a savior to rescue us from ourselves.

The Creator is not just there the first time we accept His call, but every time when we stray from the faith. When we keep our minds focused on Him, we are ready for the next step of the transformation of our hearts and souls.

* * *

As I was walking along in "Narnia," I can't say when I went from praying to yelling at God, but it happened. Getting louder and louder with my complaints against God, I'm sure that somebody else walking by would have thought I had lost my mind.

During one of these late-2008 rants, I heard a whining, droning noise from the sky above. I became irritated at the sound for interrupting my rant. I looked up to find the source of the sound (and my irritation).

There, in the sky, in white letters was written a message: *Trust Jesus!*

I looked around to see if this was some sort of joke. Maybe I was on the Truman Show. Maybe this whole thing was a prank made for TV. Maybe . . . nope, I was all alone!

I shouted loud enough to reach into the heavens, "*Really?* Is *this* your answer? My problems here are much more complicated than that. *Trust Jesus!* Is that all you have to say to me now?"

I know, it sounds a little profane as I put the words to paper. But I had heard a long time ago a youth speaker by the name of Greg Speck say, "Did it ever occur to you that nothing ever 'occurred to' God? So, you might as well be honest when you pray. God already knows what's on your mind and heart."

Saying it out loud couldn't get me into any more trouble. It was my heart. How I felt right then and there.

There was another time when Jesus told the disciples that they would make a night crossing of the Sea of Galilee while he slept in the bow of the boat. When a storm blew up, the disciples woke Jesus up in a panic and said, "Lord, save us! We're going to drown!"

Jesus had said to go over to the other side. That was His directive for that evening—not to sink halfway across and die. That was not His plan. Later, Jesus would tell them that many of them would die following Him. But not today. Today, they were just going to the other side.

Matthew 8:26 says, "He replied, 'You of little faith, why are you so afraid?' Then he got up and rebuked the winds and the waves and it was completely calm."

I love the response here in verse 27:

"The men were amazed and asked, "What kind of man is this? Even the winds and the waves obey him!"

I figured my outburst towards the heavens was okay for now. I turned my attention back to my problems and the message in the sky. I began to walk again. It didn't take long to return to my rant. This time the rant included the words in the sky above, "Trust Jesus! That's what got me into this mess!" It was then that I noticed a second message being written in the sky: A happy face drawn out, to say "Smile" and then the words "God Loves You!"

At that moment, I knew God was using a skywriter to get my attention back on Him. My trust in Jesus was at an all-time low. I was questioning if God really loved me, or if He was going to leave me to the wolves. The words of Jeremiah haunted me in that moment:

> *"For I know the plans I have for you," declares the* LORD, *"plans to prosper you and not to harm you, plans to give you hope and a future. Then you will call on me and come and pray to me, and I will listen to you. You will seek me and find me when you seek me with all your heart.*
>
> Jeremiah 29:11-13

I felt humbled, ashamed, and repentant. I knew that God had given me the Dream and vision to move to Orlando and to serve Him there. I didn't know the exact details, but I did know that God had given me just enough resources to move to the area. I had a house and I had a Bible. I could begin a Bible study for now. I just needed to get out of the boat and start walking by faith.

And so, I began yet another great adventure in my life: ministering in the shadow of Walt Disney World to people who would never make it into a church. Clearing the landscape of the huge trees of unbelief and lies, so I and others could till the hearts of many and sow the seeds of the Gospel. I reconnected with the Dream that one day there will be a harvest reaped in Orlando, Florida. This was not exactly what I had signed up for, but it was still part of the Dream that God had given me.

I had cried, "Lord, save me." I had taken my eyes off Jesus. I was more focused on the storms that surrounded me. I had lost sight of the Savior and Dream He had placed within me.

But then He snatched me from the waves. He looked me over and asked, "You of little faith, why do you doubt?" and carried me to shore.

* * *

THE DREAMER'S JOURNAL

The movie *Rocky* was the start of a $1.4 billion franchise, making Sylvester Stallone's net worth somewhere around $400 million. He has overseen eight "Rocky" movies and five Rambo movies, and he has acted in 57 movies during his career.

However, in the early '70s, Stallone was an unknown actor with minor success in the movie The Lords of Flatbush. He was broke. He had to sell his dog because he couldn't afford to feed it.

He had moved to California to pursue an acting career. It was during this time of hardship that he saw Muhammad Ali fight Chuck Wepner. In that fight, Chuck Wepner knocked down the "Greatest of all Time". Stallone later said in an interview with Forbes Magazine,[1] "And for one brief moment, this supposed stumblebum turned out to be magnificent. And he lasted and knocked the champ down. I thought if this isn't a metaphor for life."

This was the moment of Awakening for Stallone. He began writing the script for Rocky. It took him only three days to write the ninety-page script.

Stallone pitched his movie during a casting call for a different film. The producers liked it and wanted to buy the script. They offered him somewhere around $360,000 for the script, but they did not want him as the actor.

---

[1] Ward, Tom. "The Amazing Story Of The Making Of 'Rocky'." Forbes. August 29, 2017. https://www.forbes.com/sites/tomward/2017/08/29/the-amazing-story-of-the-making-of-rocky/#1f2e672a560b.

Even though he had about a hundred dollars to his name, he turned them down. He would only sell the script if he played the lead role. After some negotiation, the producers gave him $1 million to do the movie. Even in the 70's this was not much money for a movie budget. Enlisting friends, using hand-held cameras, and using only one take to film most of the movie, he came in under budget.

At the Directors Guild showing of the movie, it was clear that *Rocky* was going to special. The movie captured the hearts of critics and fans, and went on to receive nine Oscar nominations (and won three, including Best Picture). It grossed $200 million at the box office and set Sylvester Stallone on course to pursue his Dream, love his life, and live his legacy.

Here are a couple of quotes from Sylvester Stallone:

I believe there's an inner power that makes winners or losers. And the winners are the ones who really listen to the truth of their hearts.

Success is usually the culmination of controlling failure.

Could it be that Sylvester Stallone had his own encounter with the Creator who is inviting him to come to Him?

5

OBSERVING YOUR HEART: THE NEW PASSION MEANT FOR THE QUEST

Amazing grace, How sweet the sound
That saved a wretch like me . . .

"Amazing Grace" by John Newton (1779)

* * *

y Quest has not taken the most direct path. In fact, much like skipping around and reading chapters of a book out of order, my life events have been what seem to outsiders as out-of-sequence. Some very important lessons were taught to me during my teen and college experiences.

It had been a few months since the come-to-Jesus meetings I'd endured that Wednesday afternoon, when my two professors lovingly but firmly kicked my butt! During this time, I began to sense a real change in my life. I wondered if I had really changed and if the new path I was on would lead to the life I longed for?

I knew that I had experienced a clemency of sorts. I deserved to be removed from the student population of my small Christian college. While they never caught me in the act, they knew I was guilty. Some of the school leadership could sense a change within me. Others felt it was just another scam, that I was running so I could cover my crimes. Sometimes when I was alone, I would wonder which was the truth.

Was I just putting on a show for others, or had I been transformed? I did have a renewed passion to pursue the original Dream of my teenage years. But many questions consumed my thoughts. Had I drifted too far away from my Dream to find my way back? Had I crossed boundaries that would disqualify me from achieving my Dream?

All I could do now was offer myself to the Creator. I hoped that there was enough grace for me so I could pursue the Dream within my soul. Guilt was always there, drowning out the Creator's calling within my heart and soul. Even though I had goofed up, I still held onto the hope that I had not crossed the point of no return. But the grief I felt was overwhelming. I was now willing to do anything—even become a single missionary to Africa. But deep within I hoped it wouldn't come to that.

I was faced with some big decisions about my future. I was in the second half of my junior year, and I needed to finalize what degree I would graduate with, if any. I had thought about switching majors from Christian Ed./Bible to teaching so I could teach and coach. This would mean leaving my calling to ministry behind. I considered that option only because I didn't feel worthy to be anybody's pastor or even youth pastor.

What church would ever hire a youth pastor who had wasted a third of his college career chasing the very things youth pastors warn teens to stay away from? I considered teaching as a career to fall back on. While parts of it sounded good (having summers off and coaching sports teams), most of it did not sound like something I would enjoy (enforcing rules and grading papers). Of course, I could always change my major to business. But I didn't want to take accounting. The attention to detail made me a little sick to my stomach. (Kind of like when I would think about taking Greek and Hebrew to get an M. Div. and go into a pastoral role. Again, I got just a little sick to my stomach.)

Each time I made the all-in commitment to be totally and radically committed to the Creator, I would gain greater clarity about my Dream. This was true at this point in my journey too. What I really desired to do was inspire as many people as possible to follow their Dreams. I longed to motivate and guide others to not make the mistakes I had made, but to pursue their very own Dreamer's Quests. Keep the faith! Stay the course! These were the rally cries that I wanted to proclaim. But what path would best fit this Dream?

It was during this time of deep introspection that I came home to my apartment, which, to my surprise, was filled with friends (the apartment wasn't that big, so the crowd wasn't really very big either). They began to question me. They had been observing a transformation within my heart. They wondered if my transformation could somehow become an opportunity for a leadership role within the student body.

* * *

Moses is not only a foundational character for Judaism and Christianity, but also for the foundation of the laws that govern our lives today.

The Hebrew nation was transplanted to Egypt from Canaan because of famine. Joseph, one of the twelve sons of Jacob, had worked his way up from a slave to second in command of Egypt, reporting only to Pharaoh himself.

Joseph restored himself with his family (including his brothers, who had sold him into slavery). Now because of his great power and influence in Egypt, Joseph became the savior of his family by moving them to Egypt to survive the famine. It was a time of great prosperity for this family from Canaan. It allowed them to become a nation of people.

Fast forward many years, and the nation of Israel was now a political and military threat to their host nation Egypt. Pharaoh and the Egyptian people feared that Israel would one day turn on them. Pharaoh enslaved them, to work them into submission and cause their numbers to decline.

However, this plan did not work. Israel only increased in numbers and strength. So, Pharaoh resolved to defeat them. He unleashed an evil plot against the Israelite nation. He instructed the Hebrew midwives that as they delivered a Hebrews baby, they were to determine its sex. If it was a boy, they were to kill it. If it was a girl, they were to let it survive.

The Bible records that Moses was born during this dark time in Egyptian history. He was delivered in secrecy and hidden from the Egyptians. His older sister took him to the Nile River and placed him in a basket the family had made to keep the baby safe as he floated near the shore. She set the basket within the reeds to conceal the baby, but kept watch over him. Pharaoh's daughter discovered the baby and adopted him as her own. Moses, whose name means "drawn from the river," was given a place within Pharaoh's household. He was raised with the privileges of a royal family member.

As an adult, Moses discovered his true heritage. He became protective of the Hebrew people. One day he saw an overseer beating a Hebrew slave, and he stepped in to stop the abuse. The encounter ended with Moses taking the Egyptian's life. When he was found out, Moses had to leave Egypt to save his own life.

Fleeing into the desert, he encountered a group of women being taken advantage of by some men. Moses again stepped in and protected the women. This act of heroism gave Moses a position within a tribe, a wife, and a new life as a shepherd.

One day, Moses was tending his flock and had an encounter with God. God spoke to him from within a bush that burned, but was not consumed. God told Moses it was time to go back to Egypt, for He had heard the cries of His people. This time, rather than just kill one oppressor, Moses was to free the entire Hebrew nation and to lead them to the Promised Land.

Reluctantly, Moses returned to face Pharaoh. Moses became the messenger of God, through whom He sent a series of ten plagues upon Egypt. Pharaoh released the Hebrew nation. Moses led them into a wilderness area. After a miraculous escape out of Egypt, God summoned Moses to the top of a mountain to give him a set of instructions for living in their newfound freedom. This was the set of instructions for how Israel was to live in the land God had promised them.

Moses received the Ten Commandments, which became the foundation for the Mosaic Law. In many countries today, these are the same foundational laws that govern our lives. The book of Deuteronomy is the message or sermon that Moses gave the nation of Israel before they crossed the Jordan River. It was the second reading of the Law to the people. This was Moses' last opportunity to give the word of God to the people he had led.

These are the commands, decrees and laws the LORD your God directed me to teach you to observe in the land that you are crossing the Jordan to possess, so that you, your children and their children after them may fear the LORD your God as long as you live by keeping all his decrees and commands that I give you, and so that you may enjoy long life. Hear, Israel, and be careful to obey so that it may go well with you and that you may increase greatly in a land flowing with milk and honey, just as the LORD, the God of your ancestors, promised you.

Hear, O Israel: The LORD our God, the LORD is one. Love the LORD your God with all your heart and with all your soul and with all your strength. These commandments that I give you today are to be on your hearts. Impress them on your children. Talk about them when you sit at home and when you walk along the road, when you lie down and when you get up. Tie them as symbols on your hands and bind them on your foreheads. Write them on the doorframes of your houses and on your gates.

Deuteronomy 6:1-9

Let's examine the message Moses delivers here to glean some understanding of how we are to conduct ourselves when facing a major life change and transformation. We can learn much here about what it takes to move from a lifestyle of bondage to a lifestyle of freedom.

First, the rules are now shifting in a major way. The rules of your old life will no longer serve you. In the land of Ordinary, you were under a set of rules that held you in bondage. You had to conform to the will and patterns set out by those who had their best interests at heart. This rule shift is profound, and it requires a reprograming of you mind, actions, reactions and habits.

Next, we see that these laws are not just for that generation, but for every generation that will follow. This code of conduct is not just for those moving into freedom, but for those who desire to live in freedom for generations to come. This standard is not just for Moses' generation, but it is timeless and is to be passed from generation to generation. To keep from becoming enslaved again, you must pursue this standard of life.

Moses then warns that we must take great care to observe this code of conduct. He says that there are consequences that will occur if we follow this standard—blessings—and consequences if we do *not* follow this standard—not being able to enter the land of our Dream.

From here, Moses gives the first and greatest commandment: love God, the Creator, designer, and script-writer of our lives.

Devotion to God is the key to the pursuit of freedom and of our Dreams. Submission to this standard of devotion and love will be our guide to the path to fulfill our Dreams. Devotion to any other path will eventually lead us to become enslaved again to a life within Ordinary.

Finally, we see that we must communicate these standards to the next generation by modeling them. We are to lead by example. We are to live lives of freedom in front of our children, so they will know how to live in freedom. We are to talk about living our Dreams as we live in the freedom we have found in our pursuit of our own Dreams.

Moses then anticipates the normal response of anybody living in the land of Ordinary to a new set of rules.

> In the future, when your son asks you, "What is the meaning of the stipulations, decrees and laws the LORD our God has commanded you?"

Deuteronomy 6:20

In the following verses, Moses gives us the answer to the burning question we confront within our minds (and in the minds of others we try to guide into the land of their Dream): How should I live my life? For thousands of years teens have said to their parents, "Mom and Dad, that may work for you, but it doesn't work for me. Doesn't sound like freedom, either. Why should I live by your rules?" Some of you reading this book may be asking the very same question. Here's the answer:

- We are all born slaves in Ordinary. While freedom is our birthright, it is not given to us at birth. Each one of us is called by Freedom—you must answer the call. The only way to answer the call is by way of the Dreamer's Quest. The only way to flourish in the new life of freedom is to adapt to new rules. These are the rules of freedom and not of bondage. These are the rules to your Awakening.

- By answering the call of the Creator and following the Creator's rules, you will embark upon the Dreamer's Quest. The calling and the rules become your road-map out of Ordinary (bondage) and into your Dream (extraordinary freedom to be who you are really meant to be!).

- These are the rules to receiving miraculous and extraordinary blessings in life.

- This new way of living is the path to increased influence, impact, and income.

- Embarking upon the Dreamer's Quest and fulfilling the Creator's intent for your life will become your legacy. This is the path that will lead to loving your life and living your legacy today!

When we move from the land beyond the Dream Gate and enter the Believe Gate, we encounter a conflict between two very different systems of observing the world.

One system is the system of the masses. It is the system of Ordinary, and its rules rely on conforming to the pattern that everybody else lives by. It's the pattern that demands you follow the herd, even when the herd is racing on a path to destruction.

This path of the herd is lined with ideas that are *almost* right. Take, for instance, "Do your own thing," or "Majority rules," or "Might makes right." While there are elements of truth within them, they fail to provide the complete truth, leaving the believers of these statements enslaved in the land of Ordinary. As we uncover these falsehoods that have led us astray, we begin to reveal more about the Creator and His plans for our lives:

- "Do your own thing" becomes "Do what Creator has designed for you as a special and important person within His plan." Your purpose in life becomes your own, because you are designed by the Creator to achieve this purpose.

- "Majority rules" becomes "The Creator directs our paths into freedom."

- "Might makes right" becomes "The might of a loving Creator makes everything right."

The Creator's system is a path to extraordinary activity. This path allows us to pursue the design the Creator has given us and the story He has placed us within. It is a path that is lined with thoughts such as:

- My design is to serve others.

- We all were once slaves to Ordinary, needing to break free of our numbness.

- I must use my newfound power to guide others to reach their potential.

Here in the land of Believe, you are confronted with a choice. Are you going to believe the system of bondage that you left behind in Ordinary? Or are you going to Believe the message of freedom and follow the path of the Dreamer's Quest?

* * *

I was happy to see each of these old friends in my apartment, however unexpected their presence was. I had cut ties with them eighteen months before because I knew they would not have approved of my behavior. I had cut off all contact with them—I knew they would confront me if I kept them in my life. In the last couple of months, I'd been too ashamed to reenter my close-knit group of friends. I was worried this would be another come-to-Jesus meeting, but the smiles and greetings I received told me it was something different. Something I didn't deserve, but that I had longed for: acceptance back into the old gang.

"Did you know that tomorrow is the student body election?" asked one of my oldest friends.

"Yeah, now that you mention it." I replied.

"What do you think of the guys running for President?"

"I really don't know them. I guess we will have to choose one of them. Why? Which one do you guys think we should vote for?" I didn't know where this was going. Had I offended one of the candidates? In my rebellion, had I done something to one of them that now required restitution? My mind raced as I tried to sort out why everybody was in my apartment.

"We have been thinking. We feel you would make a much better president than either of them. Would you consider accepting the role of student body president if it was offered to you?" All the others nodded in agreement.

My first thought was, *Are they playing a big a prank on me, or the students and administration?* My second thought was, *What is their plan?* The election was tomorrow. Even if I agreed to run for student body president, did the idea have any chance for success? Finally, I thought, *Why me?* Was I worthy to put my name in the running?

After they convinced me to move forward with this radical idea, we quickly disbanded to execute an unlikely plan. They were going to do this. This was no joke. They believed I would be a better candidate than the other two other guys running for office.

The first and only "Phil for President" meeting concluded with a simple but crazy plan to market a write-in candidate overnight. They would cover the entire campus with three-by-five notecards. On the cards was a simple message: *Phil Johnson—Write-In Candidate for Student Body President.*

When my friends asked me to consider their offer to campaign for me, I questioned my worthiness as a candidate. As they laid out the merits they saw in me, it was humbling. I had such low estimation of myself at the time. I did not feel worthy of their endorsement, nor of their forgiveness. In my rebellion, I had treated them (and many others) horribly.

Rather than seeing a guy who had blown it, they saw a guy God was working on, for whom the best was yet to come. They saw leadership where I saw failure. They saw potential where I saw waste. Finally, they saw a person who could relate to most everybody where I saw a person who had burned too many bridges to make a difference anymore.

I gave my approval, not really believing I could win. The next morning, I made my way across campus to a sight that blew me away (and thinking about it, to this day, still does). Because of my friends' late-night efforts, my name and my intention to be the next student body president were plastered everywhere I looked. I had just about everybody greeting me with either "Good job," "Go for it," or "Are you really running? Okay, good!"

I didn't want to get my hopes too high. My election committee told me their polling looked really good. *Okay,* I tried to comfort myself. *I guess I won't be a joke, but can I really win?*

The next morning, I was awakened by a phone call. It was college president Dr. Welch's office calling, asking me to come directly to his office for a meeting. Oh boy, I hadn't counted on that one. As I showered, I wondered what one wears to meet with the president of one's college. I didn't ever remember speaking to him before.

The next couple of hours were much like the two meetings with my professors that I had endured several months before. I was in the woodshed, taking my licks, again. Not only was Dr. Wilbert Welch there, but Dr. Warren Fabor, the vice-president, and the Dean of Students, Noe Palacios, were also in attendance. I was questioned thoroughly. A senator on the judiciary committee didn't have anything over these three men's interrogation abilities. The lines of questioning were direct, pointed, and somewhat brutal. They began to go point-by-point through the code of conduct—citing suspicions about my activities, but never accusing me of anything directly. I endured this for about an hour and a half. By the end of the meeting, I was dripping with sweat and was totally wrung out. I wished I had worn workout shorts and a T-shirt instead of my suit.

During the meeting, they mentioned that I had won by a very wide margin. While I would never know the exact numbers, the other two candidates had not been able to pull together much more than 25 or 30 percent of the vote between them. However, I had violated the procedures to run for president. There were applications and interviews and approvals that I had bypassed with my write-in campaign. I had to answer for this breach of conduct. I also had to answer to the rumors about my conduct for the last eighteen months. While they had no solid proof of my missteps, they knew I had plenty.

Towards the end of our meeting, the three men focused on the mercy afforded by God and His grace to all of us. Forgiveness was an important concept to these men, even while holding the highest of standards. However, my waste of leadership potential was almost too much for them to overcome. They, like many others who had been watching me, had seen something in me that I didn't see in myself—potential. But I needed to repent and to redirect my path if I was serious about this leadership role. I assured them that I was prepared to meet the challenge.

So, a plan was hatched in the president's office that morning. I wasn't allowed to weigh in on this plan, but I did see how leadership worked at the highest levels of the college. Dr. Welch was concerned about the integrity of the institution and its standards and methods. Dr. Fabor was concerned with my advancement on my journey towards leadership. Noe Palacios had the interests of the student body at the forefront of his mind.

Together, they determined that I would, in fact, file the application to be student body president. I would be examined by a committee. I would also present a speech to the student body, asking forgiveness for my radical methods, giving my vision for the coming year, and asking for their votes in a runoff election between me and the second-place candidate. The second election would take place the next day. All three men had their fingerprints on this plan, and I only had to agree to it. I did.

After my application was properly filed, my interviews completed, and my speech given (as well as the other candidates'), we voted again. I won—again.

It would take me many years to realize how much I grew in those next fifteen months. I had regular meetings with Dr. Welch and Noe Palacios, who both sharpened me to become a better version of myself. I sat on the judiciary committee that was tasked with the discipleship of students. That taught me how to approach difficult matters. I spoke and led at campus events, student body meetings, chapels, and fund-raisers. I included everybody in the process, which was considered *way* outside of ordinary practices. Because I was given this opportunity, I wanted to share it with as many people as possible, giving them the same advantage and access to leadership that I had been given.

I had been wondering for some time if I had experienced transformation in the spring of 1981. By the fall of 1982, I was convinced that I had, as I completed my education and leadership experience, made plans to become a youth pastor, and married the woman of my dreams. I wouldn't change a thing, even though I regret my rebellion against God's calling to the Dream he had designed for me. I had to go through all of it to get to where I am today.

Life doesn't happen *to* you. It happens *for* you! Give in to your transformation!

* * *

THE DREAMER'S JOURNAL

John Newton was born in 1725, in a district of London called Wapping, near the Thames River. His father was a shipping merchant who was at sea most of the time. John's mother died when he was six years old, and he spent most of his childhood at boarding school or in the care of a distant step-mother. For most of his childhood John Newton was mistreated.

At age eleven, he joined his father at sea as an apprentice. However, he was headstrong and disobedient, which only worsened his life of troubles. He came close to death on several occasions. Once, during his youth, he examined his relationship with the Creator and decided to turn away from Him.

Newton became known for his bad habits. His bad behavior would eventually end his service of the Royal Navy. He later deserted from there to pursue the woman he would one day marry, Mary "Polly" Catlett. Because of this desertion, he was moved into service on a slave ship.

Newton would mock the captain by writing obscene poems and songs about him. These obscene works became popular among the crew, who would sing and chant them openly. This led to further confrontations, and his behavior got him imprisoned while at sea and almost cost him his life. Newton's father intervened on his behalf, and he moved to the ship *Greyhound*. There he continued exercising his talent for writing obscene poems and inventing new profanities. The captain said John was the most profane man he'd ever met.

It was upon the *Greyhound,* in a terrible storm in the North Sea, that John Newton met death once again. After cursing the storm and tying himself to a pump so he would not be washed overboard, he cried out "If this will not do, Lord, have mercy upon us!" He spent the next eleven hours on deck steering the ship, thinking about his prayer of conversion.

Before he left the sea for good, it would take several more years serving as captain on slave ships, with the promise that one day he would become the captain of a ship with cargo that was unrelated to slavery. It was after another collapse in his health that took him from the sea.

During this time, he had courted his wife-to-be. After leaving the sea, he took her in marriage and became a customs agent in Liverpool. There he began to study theology, Latin, and Greek. He soon caught the attention of many, and some suggested that he become a priest in the Church of England. However, being turned down for his lack of formal education, Newton continued his personal studies and wrote about his experiences in the slave trade and his conversion. After years of study, he was offered a position in a church as the curacy of Olney, Buckinghamshire in 1764.

From the pulpit, John Newton would share his personal story, which was a refreshing departure from the norm for listeners. It was during this time, wanting to share how God's grace and mercy extend to all, that he wrote the words to "Amazing Grace."

6

OBSERVING YOUR SOUL: THE NEW PURPOSE INTENDED FOR THE QUEST

You can have everything in life you want, if you will just help other people get what they want.

Zig Ziglar (1926-2012)

* * *

We would call it a black hole. You would pass the basketball to a player, and you'd never see it again. They would either shoot the ball or turn it over to the other team. Even if there was another player open who had a shot, they would try to make the play all by themselves. Their behavior hurt every player on the team, including themselves.

I have seen this play out not only on the playgrounds and sport teams of my youth, but in ministries, churches, and businesses. You know what I'm talking about: that one person who is not only in it to win it, but to win it all for themselves. All the fame, the glory, the money, and the power—they want it all for themselves.

If I'm honest, I've had some issues loving black-hole people. At first, everything looks like it's going to be great and like everybody loves everybody. Then the struggles begin as you divide the leadership, the center of attention, the recognition, or the earnings. When the expectations of a self-centered individual surface, greedy and selfish actions are sure to follow. All that follows is a mess for somebody else to throw out or clean up.

These people will cause division, taint the truth about themselves and others, and cause a wave of negativity to wash over the organization. What was once a great opportunity is now a drain on every facet of your life. Your emotions are on the ragged edge. You begin to think in an unhealthy manner. The opportunity for success is lost. It does not matter if you hoped to advance your finances or your career, or to fulfill your life's Dream; it is all in jeopardy now. Like a real black hole, these people have a gravity that draws negativity to them, and that negativity orbits them.

However, the true nature of our Dreamer's Quest is not getting more for yourself. It is all about giving as much as possible to as many as possible. The world is waiting for you to take center stage of your Dream: not so you can cash in, but so you will be free to serve. Free to assist others with their Awakenings! It is when we encourage, support, and motivate others that we will find the purpose we seek. You must pass the ball and be part of a successful team!

Kary Oberbrunner has guided me on my Dreamer's Quest. He is an author, coach and speaker who has guided thousands to find clarity, competence, confidence, impact, influence and income. His coaching and books have become the foundation for my path and is found throughout this book. One of the most important quotes I have taken from him is this: "Show up filled up!"

This short but powerful message sums up the antidote to being a black hole. First, to be successful in life you must show up! Many of us don't even show up on the court to receive that pass. Our spot on the team is vacant. The world is waiting for you to take your spot on the court.

Second, you need to take your place filled up! If they do show up to take their place on the court, many are only there to get—not to give. In fact, they show up out of shape, not ready to play as part of the team.

I ran an open gym in Columbus, Ohio for about six years. Every Sunday afternoon, I would open the gym for anybody who would like to come in and play basketball. It was a ministry I inherited from others who had been doing this for many years. It had become a place where some of the best basketball talent in the area would come and play.

I would try to keep up with these young men. Many played on high school and college teams. Various leagues used the Sunday gym time as a fun way to sharpen their skills for other more important outings. For others, like myself, it was a way to hang onto a game they had loved in high school and college. I would play with them every week. Out of shape and getting slower every year, I had a harder and harder time keeping up. Usually, the only reason they would let me play was because I had the keys to the gym.

Almost every week, one or two new guys would come in to show off their talents. They needed to prove that they were the best in the gym. They would be the black holes for the day. Nobody wanted to play with them. Sometimes the black holes would come in groups of five so they could better showcase their abilities. The other guys were there only to pass the ball to them.

I had set up play so they had to mix it up. No standing teams. No dominating the court with endless wins, never coming off to let others play. We wouldn't let a team stay on the court for more than three wins. There was a sign-up list, and the next five names would become the next team. I would place my name in the middle of the names to break them up. Most of them didn't like it, but it was my gym and my rules.

I would walk up to the black hole who was now on my team, shake their hand, and say "Hi, my name is Phil. All you need to know about me is that I am always hot and I'm always open. So, pass me the ball!"

Taken aback, many would give me a look and say nothing. Some would challenge me. But all would understand my message: *There are no black holes here.* Everybody is here to have a great time. It is so much fun to play with people that draw out the best in you. It's not fun to play with people who only want to show off their skills. It is great to have a great player on your team, somebody you can count on to make the big play. But it is not fun (and many times not successful) to play with one guy dominating the team. Why should I play defense and make stops when I am not any part of the scoring at the other end?

After a couple of trips up and down the court, the black hole players would see that I was more about making a great pass than making the shot to win the game. And that philosophy became the culture of the gym. *Make the great pass. Set the great pick. Play the best defense. Show up filled up. Come to give, not to get. It's more fun that way!*

Submitting to one another out of reverence for Christ.

Ephesians 5:21

The Creator is the inspiration for the servant leadership movement. It is a philosophy that many express adherence to, but few achieve the level of servanthood required to be a true servant leader. Some of the best-known advocates of this philosophy are spectacular teachers, but fall short in their execution of servant leadership.

Jesus Christ was the author of servant leadership. He spoke against leaders who misused their authority for personal gain.

He taught that this is not true of the Dreamer who is on the right Quest. To achieve your true destiny, he taught, become a servant to all by doing what you are designed to be:

> *Jesus called them together and said, "You know that those who are regarded as rulers of the Gentiles lord it over them, and their high officials exercise authority over them. Not so with you. Instead, whoever wants to become great among you must be your servant, and whoever wants to be first must be slave of all. For even the Son of Man did not come to be served, but to serve, and to give his life as a ransom for many."*

> Mark 10:42-45

It would have been one thing just to teach this model to His disciples. However, Jesus allowed the authorities to arrest Him and place Him before false accusers and an unjust legal system to be convicted and executed. Why? To pay the penalty we all have incurred by our neglect of the design and script the Creator gave us. We can pursue our Dreams only because Jesus Christ showed up on earth filled up with love and grace. He qualifies us to become the people we are designed to be. Because of the servant leadership of Jesus Christ, we are no longer disqualified or under penalty of death.

> *The thief comes only to steal and kill and destroy; I have come that they may have life and have it to the full.*

> John 10:10

Jesus taught this model and put it into action.

> *fixing our eyes on Jesus, the pioneer and perfecter of faith. For the joy set before him he endured the cross, scorning its shame, and sat down at the right hand of the throne of God.*

> Hebrews 12:2

To climb Mount Everest, you need a guide to get you to the top. To accomplish great things, you need to follow those who have achieved greatness. You must follow a great guide to get where you want to go in life. Today we call them mentors. In the Jewish culture of the Bible, they referred to them as "Rabbi." A student would refer to this person as their teacher or professor.

In Paul's letter to the church in Philippi, a first-century church located in the Macedonian region, he speaks of how his chains have advanced the gospel. Most importantly, Paul points the church towards imitation of Christ's humility. Most likely, the letter that Paul penned was written about ten years after his visit to the Philippians, while he was being held as prisoner of the state in Rome.

In your relationships with one another, have the same mindset as Christ Jesus:

> *Who, being in very nature God,*
> *did not consider equality with God something to be used to*
> *his own advantage;*
> *rather, he made himself nothing*
> *by taking the very nature of a servant,*
> *being made in human likeness.*
> *And being found in appearance as a man,*
> *he humbled himself*
> *by becoming obedient to death—*
> *even death on a cross!"*

Philippians 2:5-8

Paul knew that this young church needed a mentor. Paul used not only his hardships to inspire this church, but he also used the life and ministry of Jesus Christ. The example of Jesus serves as the North Star of believers. The writer of the book of Hebrews carries on this theme:

Therefore, since we are surrounded by such a great cloud of witnesses, let us throw off everything that hinders and the sin that so easily entangles. And let us run with perseverance the race marked out for us, [2] fixing our eyes on Jesus, the pioneer and perfecter of faith. For the joy set before him he endured the cross, scorning its shame, and sat down at the right hand of the throne of God. [3] Consider him who endured such opposition from sinners, so that you will not grow weary and lose heart.

Hebrews 12:1-3

The writer here gives a nod to the many great leaders who have gone before us in the Christian faith. Because of the "great cloud of witnesses," we are to set aside anything that would hinder or entangle us on our Dreamer's Quest. But the writer goes on to offer an even greater example of how we are to live our lives: Jesus Christ. Here, Jesus is described as the "pioneer and perfecter" of the faith. The instruction here is to enter the journey with joy, endurance, honor, strength, resolution, and character, just like Jesus did.

Whatever term you use, it is important that you follow a mentor, teacher, or a leader who will "show up filled up." Why? Because a student becomes just like their teacher. We used to say it this way: "More is caught than taught." You take on the personality of the person who is molding you. Care should be taken to match your desired goals with the mentors you select.

Next, you must make sure that you are serving the people around you. Are you showing up filled up, or do you show up to get and not to give? This is in direct opposition to what the culture says about getting ahead in life. You have heard that you must watch out for yourself. While there is some truth in that statement, if you don't make others a priority, then you will find yourself drifting into the selfish waters of greed and excess.

* * *

The year 1982 changed my life. Sandy Sanders became my bride in October. At the same time, I was finishing the last two classes for my degree. Sandy and I had taken two weeks in the middle of that semester to get married and take a honeymoon. (It was great for us as a couple, but not so great for my academic career.)

I fulfilled all my requirements for my degree program in December. After I completed my program, we moved back to our hometown to continue the search for a youth pastor position. It was difficult to send Sandy off to work every day while I sat at home, writing letters, making phone calls, and waiting to hear back from churches. She had a great job at the sheriff's department. I waited for the phone to ring and the mail to come every day. After six months of phone calls and interviews, I was selected to be youth pastor at the Fremont Grace Brethren Church in Ohio.

On June 1, 1983, I moved into my first office. It was a beautiful office with a full wall of windows facing south. I had a view of farms, beyond the church parking lot as far as I could see. Another wall was devoted to bookshelves. My small library would have to grow to fill that whole wall. I had a huge desk and several office chairs for guest and two filing cabinets. But what really blew me away with was the chair behind the desk. It was an executive high-back chair. This gave my office—and me, I hoped—a note of gravitas.

It took me about thirty minutes to get my small collection of books and files moved into this impressive space. Just outside my door was the church secretary's office. Like me, she was in her twenties, but she seemed to be on top of everything. There was also another secretary who had been the only one in the office for years. She came in a day or two each week to make sure the operation was running smoothly. You could tell she had all the details in her head. She was very willing to guide me in the right direction.

After moving into my office that June morning, I sat in silence. For the first time in my life, I was pursuing my Dream—for real this time. This wasn't a dress rehearsal. This was the main event.

As I sat there, a little excited but a little fearful, something occurred to me. *Now what? What am I supposed to do now?* It was in that moment that I realized that I was totally unprepared for what was going to happen next. I had a degree in Bible, Christian Education, and Youth Ministry. I had been a youth intern since my high school years. But I had no idea of where I wanted to lead this group of teens. All I knew was that they needed a leader. They needed someone to guide them during this very important time in life. But I wasn't sure what that looked like. I had some great examples of youth leaders in my past, but I never really understood their reasons for doing everything they did. I could fill a calendar with activities, but why was I scheduling them in the first place?

I went back to my most basic understanding of ministry. I was there to serve the teens, their parents, and the staff. I needed to get to know them. *I know*, I thought. *I'll invite them for root beer floats at the A&W down the street.* I called the church secretary into my newly arranged office, with my modest library behind me, and asked how we could invite every teen to meet one on one with me as soon as possible. She knew way more than I realized. She listened to my idea and guided me to write up what I had in mind. She then took my hand-written ideas and created my first newsletter. She put the newsletter into the mail (remember, it was 1983 and this was fast-paced, high-tech stuff back then. She even had some clip art that we copied and pasted by hand to make it look hip!).

Soon the phone began to ring. It was teens from the church, asking how they could redeem the coupon for a free root beer float that had appeared in the newsletter. The secretary took the calls and made appointments for me. Sometimes she stacked them back-to-back, so I would enjoy two or three root beers, shakes, or floats in one afternoon. Sometimes it was just one guy; other times it was a group of three to five girls. The time with the guys was filled with long periods of silence. The time with the girls was an information overload. I learned so much during these encounters. My biggest takeaway was that the students in the church felt unwanted. They just needed somebody to make them a priority—somebody to serve them.

I wanted to let them know I was here, and that I was here to serve them. The meetings at the A&W laid the groundwork for relationships that have lasted for thirty-plus years. Some of them are friends I can count on to this day. For others, I am still their youth pastor.

I am so glad I didn't stay in that office too long. In fact, most of my memories of Fremont didn't take place in that office. They took place in camps and campgrounds, rivers, buses, vans, amusement parks, malls, barns, and fields. I remember the youth rooms we built together. And I remember the brown picnic table that I sat at drinking root beer that hot summer in 1983.

You see, I didn't show up to get a nice office or a big salary (we never made over $20,000 a year, and we never had health insurance—but that's another story, for another time, about God's provision). I had come to help the students to begin their very own Dreamer's Quests. I came to help spark their Awakenings—their Awakenings to the possibilities of the greatness within them.

Don't be a black hole player in life: the type of person who only looks to show off your God-given talents to advance your reputation. That person who uses their skills to increase their standing in the community. The individual that applies their resources to create security for only themselves. Your Dream is given to you to serve others. Don't waste it on serving only yourself.

I don't care if you say "Show up filled up," or "Come to give and not to get." It is all the same thing. It's the servant leadership model. We are to follow the example of Jesus and to serve the world with our gift.

* * *

THE DREAMER'S JOURNAL

Zig Ziglar was a struggling door-to-door salesman until he found a simple formula for success: listen and learn from Jesus Christ and others who are successful in life.

Zig was born in Coffee County, Alabama. In 1931, when Zig was five years old, his father moved his wife and their twelve kids to Yazoo City Mississippi. (Zig was the tenth of the twelve children.) However, a year later, his father died of a stroke. One of his sisters died a few days later. His mother, Lila, had a powerful impact on his life as she raised twelve children during the Great Depression and faced the loss of her husband and daughter. Later Zig would quote many of her timeless truths, such as, "It's not who's right that's important; it's what's right," "The person who won't stand for something will fall for anything," and "If you set the example, you will not have to set the rules." These quotes from Zig's mother were the foundation of many of his seminars that would inspire millions to rise to the top of their field.

Ziglar served in the Navy. Upon coming out, he got married and tried his hand at a college education. This did not work out for him. As he put it, "I was the part of the class that makes the top half possible." He left college and become a door-to-door cookware salesman. For two years he struggled. Knowing he had to stay positive to stay a salesman, he would dress up every morning and kiss his wife goodbye. He made sure to keep a smile and a positive attitude. He was able to become a pretty good salesman by age twenty-five and was promoted to divisional sales supervisor.

It was during this period that Zig heard his first motivational speaker. He had never seen anybody do something that appeared to be so fun and to make such a huge impact. He knew it was what he wanted to do. Keeping his day job, he began to speak for free to churches, civic organizations, and clubs. He put together some of his and his mother's sayings and learned the joys of speaking.

By the time of his death, he had spoken in person to millions of people. He had sold millions of books and tens of millions of audio recordings (first phonographs, then tapes, and then CDs). He was worth around $15 million. His children have kept his vision alive by taking his message to the next generation—to inspire others to the greatness the Creator has placed within them.

All of this was built on his philosophy: "You can have everything in life you want, if you will just help other people get what they want." In other words, arrive ready to give and not to get (or show up filled up)! The Creator gave you your very own Dreamer's Quest. You have been Awakened to serve, not to be served.

PART 3

To Dare—Affecting!

It isn't long before Tripp comes across the third gate. As he gets closer, he reads the word *Dare* carved into the gate. It appears that the letters have been chopped into the wooden structure—like something you would see in an Old West frontier fort. The word *Dare* seems to have been hastily carved with quick strokes from an ax or a hatchet. However, as he inspects the rough and crude gate more closely, he sees the beautiful workmanship which reads *To Master with Confidence,* hand-carved into the door.

Tripp reaches within his pack to retrieve the old mask he wore in Ordinary. He is filled with an empty sense of false security as he places the mask on, hoping to relieve some of his anxiety.

There, camped at the entrance, Tripp recognizes the Traveler who guided him to the first two gates. She walks toward him as soon as she sees him coming toward the gate. She asks him quickly and directly:

"Have you begun your transformation into who the Creator has designed you to be?"

"I think so . . . uh . . . yes! I have." Tripp answers, taken aback by her directness.

The Traveler gazes into his eyes, saying nothing. It is not a gaze of doubt or of judgment, but of inquiry to understand Tripp's readiness for what lies ahead.

Tripp breaks the silence and the inspection. "I am focused on the Dream now. I have left Ordinary behind to follow my Dream. I now believe in my design and the story the Creator has entrusted me with. I am totally and radically committed to my Awakening! The more I learn what to Believe about my Dream, the greater clarity I gain. Oh, one more important belief that has surprised me: I have been given this Dream to serve others."

"Okay, that sounds good. Are you ready to put that to the test? To step into the trials that will determine if you really believe everything you just said?" the Traveler asks. Tripp's soul is immediately alerted to the insightfulness of the experienced Traveler. Her eyes are piercing beyond the mask he threw on when he saw her to cover the doubt that he still carried. It was a look that pierces deep within his soul. But it was also a look of both determination *and* compassion. Tripp feels both a connection of a kindred spirit and the awe of being in the presence of a battle-tested warrior. It is like she knows what is ahead and that it will take courage to move forward in this Quest, but that it will also introduce a price that must be paid—a very high price.

"Lose the mask." The Traveler orders. "It's not fooling anybody. Besides, it makes you look silly."

Tripp pauses. Has he learned enough to move forward? Is he ready to be put to the test? What if he fails and he loses his Dream forever? But what good is his Dream doing him if he does not enter the gate, but remains here in this land that is devoted to learning about the rules to pursue the Dream? He had been instructed that the path to accomplishing the Dream is beyond this gate.

What really haunts him is the revealing that begins when he walks up to the gate. It is like all the masks that Tripp has used to cover his pain and emptiness are being torn away, and he is standing naked before the world. This causes a fear to shoot straight to his soul. But that fear is met by the clarity of his Dream and the convictions of his beliefs. Tripp knows that he is designed by the Creator to move forward. His masks are false security to cover his fear.

It is a very strange, unfamiliar struggle that rages within his mind. He knows he could give way to either side in this moment. *Is* he ready to put his commitment to the test? He ponders the Traveler's question, "Are you ready to put your beliefs to the test?" He blurts out his answer:

"Yes!" Tripp replies. Quickly he removes his mask and places it back into his pack. The Traveler looks at him with a smirk and shakes her head.

"If you feel you must carry that along, that's up to you. But my advice is that you lighten your load before you pass through the gate." Tripp nods that he hears her, but he closes his pack without removing the mask.

"Okay then, let's move out." She points to the Gate. "By the way, my name is Alva. It is an honor to fight alongside you."

Tripp has known her name from the lectures she gave in the halls behind them. Her talks were both inspiring and informative. He has researched her adventures, and while she is not famous like some, her Dreamer's Quest is captivating. Tripp knows she is someone he can trust. However, the word "fight" rings in Tripp's head. *Fight! What have I gotten myself into here?*

"Oh, my name is Tripp," he replies to Alva. "What do you mean when you say 'fight?'"

Alva smiles the same smile she gave him before. "This land is the land of your pain. You must learn the skill to overcome the roadblocks, self-limiting beliefs, and doubts that will deter you from your Quest. You are now in the land of the battles for your mind, your emotions, and your will. This is a battle zone, a land where you must conquer the enemies of your Dream."

Tripp nods as he steps forward. He feels a surge of fear overcome his soul again. Alva passes weapons to him, which he tucks away into his belt. She explains each weapon and its use as she passes them to him. The first is a sword. Alva explains that the name of this sword is "truth," and he is to use it to defeat lies. The next is a shield. Alva goes on to explain that the shield is to be used in battles when arrows begin to fly. In this land, the arrows are called "doubts," and they will come from all directions—"So be alert and use the shield often!" she says. The third is in a small pouch. She explains that the pouch contains the details of Tripp's assignment and why he was selected for this mission.

A rush of adrenaline runs through Tripp's body. It is the same fear that held him at the entrance of the Dream Gate for months. He fears that his face will betray him. He quickly looks away to hide his fear.

"I see you are already under attack, and we haven't even crossed through the gate yet. Quickly, repeat your beliefs again out loud." Alva says, unfazed by the fear building within her travel companion.

Tripp repeats, "I am focused on the Dream. I have left Ordinary. I believe that my design and my story the Creator has given are true. I am totally and radically committed to my Awakening! I have been given this Dream to serve, not to be served."

Just as they begin to move forward, out of the memories of leaving Ordinary, he sees a close family member and a friend. Both have tears of betrayed loved ones flowing down their faces, which quickly turn to red-faced rage as they shout, "Stop! You are going the wrong way. Ordinary is back this way. Please, don't throw your life away!"

Feeling a pull within his soul drawing him back to Ordinary, he freezes in place. Alva spins him around to face her. She looks into his eyes with compassion and determination.

"Tell me again what have you learned!" Alva demands.

Tripp repeats, "I am focused on the Dream. I have left Ordinary. I believe my design and my story. I am totally and radically committed! I have been given this Dream to serve!"

They are now on the move, passing through the gate into what looks like a battle. The arrows that Alva called "doubts" are coming from every direction. Tripp clumsily hides himself behind the shield Alva had given him and awkwardly follows. As he tries to speak, his mind races with thoughts of retreat, fear, and defeat. He hears voices! Voices of family and close friends surface to the forefront of his mind. These voices, which once were such a comfort to him back in Ordinary, are now telling him this is the biggest mistake of his life.

Just inside the gate, Tripp is shocked. He envisions even more family and friends beckoning him to return to Ordinary. Some weep, and some hurl insults and anger his way. He has been building courage and confidence, but the pain of rejection cuts deep into his soul.

"The pouch! Read the words of your mission and your value! Do it now!" Alva shouts as they move forward.

As Tripp repeats the words out loud, he thinks to himself, *You are in over your head. What were you thinking?*

In time, Trip learns how to handle the gifts that Alva gave him. He has acquired the skills to slay foes that spit out lies in his direction with the sword of truth. He is now able to protect himself from the arrows of doubt with the shield given to him. He has memorized the words upon the paper held within the pouch, but he never sets out in any direction without consulting the words contained upon the pages.

Tripp is now in the land of Dare. He is learning how to put belief into action. He is learning to master the voices, distractions, and self-limiting beliefs so he can move beyond this land and into the land of his Dream.

7

DARE TO DISCERN YOUR GATEKEEPERS: THE WELL-INTENTIONED CRITICS

There will be haters, there will be doubters, there will be non-believers, and then there will be you proving them wrong.

Jennifer Van Allen

* * *

I love people. I love interacting with people, meeting new people, learning their stories, and connecting their stories with mine. I love finding openings into people's souls and helping them discover their Dreams. I love serving them with my gifts and encouraging them to grow in their love for their personal Dreamer's Quests. I love to see transformation in others—whether I had a part in it, or am just hearing the story. I love people.

At the same time, I don't always *like* people. While many are well-intentioned, some, even those close to you, can be very critical. As a young youth pastor, I had not been warned of the assaults that would come from the very people I'd be ministering to. The criticisms came in rapid succession from those who I thought would give me the greatest praise. It blew me away. I questioned myself, my purpose, my calling, my Dream. I wanted to retreat back to the land of Ordinary.

The well-intending critics would line up to give conflicting advice that would shake the confidence of any rational person:

- "You're too spiritual."

- "You're not spiritual enough."

- "You are a control freak."

- "You don't know what you are doing—you're out of control."

- "You have too many rules."

- "You don't have enough rules."

- "You are controlled by your plans and you don't care about us personally."

- "You have not done enough planning."

It was during one of these very challenging moments, when I was being hit from all sides, that a well-intentioned critic entered my office unannounced.

Early on as a youth pastor, I had taken to heart many of the challenges Christian singer-songwriter Keith Green had proclaimed in his concerts, songs, and book. By faith, he would rent out concert halls, school gyms, and any other place he could afford to hold a concert. He did not charge for his performances. He would take a "love offering" during the concert, asking attendants to give so he could reach more people with the gospel. At the concerts, he would only suggest a price for his music and books, letting many take these items home for free. He would only suggest that some should give more for these resources to help pay for others who needed to hear the message.

He would forbid gifts from those who did not believe. He felt it was wrong to charge for sharing the Gospel, which is a gift without any charge from God. It didn't make sense to him to charge somebody to hear about a gift. I agreed.

I decided that I would not charge anything (or as little as possible) for any event I ran in my youth ministry. It was a belief that would become a game-changer for myself and for my ministries through the years. If I did have to charge a fee, I would do everything in my power to make it as inexpensive as possible. Further, I would not charge my youth volunteers: they would attend camps, conferences and events at no charge. I was asking my volunteer staff to take time off work and to be away from family to attend these functions. It did not make sense to charge them to attend. I built all my ministries upon this principle for many years. However, I couldn't always drive costs down as much as I wanted to.

There were times when I would struggle to balance the need to charge for an event with my desire to allow everybody to attend at no or low cost. There were times when I had to decide who would get the greater assistance: the volunteers or the students. Back to the encounter in my office with the well-intentioned parent.

I had hoped that we would become friends. I had hoped he would become a mentor of mine, guiding me in the business side of ministry. His leadership within his ministry was well-known, and I admired his skills. However, I was never able to break free of the barrier placed between us.

As I listened to his eruption of raw emotion, I tried to hear what had set this powder keg off. He confronted me about the price I had set for students to attend a weeklong youth conference. My pricing was higher than what the sponsoring organization had posted on their website for this event. I had factored in transportation, conference tickets, and the cost to take along volunteer staff, whom I did not charge to attend (there was a minimum requirement of adult staff needed to chaperone the teens).

If I remember correctly, there was a $50 to $75 upcharge per student, making our cost around $600 per student. For our youth group to attend, I had to have a student to adult ratio of 12 to 1. Another factor: the cost of transportation was high since the conference was on the other side of the country. I spent hours searching for the best options for transportation. The final factor was that my budget was low that year.

I knew that this number would be a burden for some of our students. I told the whole youth group that if money was the only reason holding them back from attending, they could come see me and I would work something out with them (I knew that I could approach individuals in our church who would sponsor students to attend).

All this parent saw was the price differences between my advertised cost to attend the event and the sponsoring organization's quoted price. He would not take my explanation seriously. The parent accused me of being a thief, taking advantage of the students. He said that I was taking the money to fund a vacation for my staff and myself. That I was not qualified to be a youth pastor or any other kind of pastor. According to him, I was a liar. I was a prideful and arrogant man who was preying upon students. He demanded that I resign immediately from the pastorate and leave the church.

I was deeply cut by his words!

I sat in stunned silence after the encounter. I had lost all confidence in my Dream, my life's calling, and myself. This man's words, along with the words of other family and friends, haunted me for years. I could hear them in moments when I needed to take a risk. I would second-guess my decisions because I would remember the accusations that I was a thief. The thought, *I should get a real job* would come to me as I stepped in front of a group to speak. I found myself in the land of Dare, looking for the confidence to keep moving forward. Did I have the courage to continue my Dreamer's Quest?

* * *

THE PATIENCE OF JOB

Job was a very successful man by almost any standards. According to the opening passage in the book that bears his name, he was a man of character, a man with a large family, and a businessman of great personal wealth. He was considered the greatest man in the East during a time of great prosperity in that region. He was also the spiritual leader of his family, making sure that not only he, but also his children, were pure before God. He was the total package.

After introducing the leading man, the book of Job cuts away to a conversation in heaven between God and Satan. God pointed out Job as an example of what it looks like to be a true worshiper of Him. Satan questioned Job's character and integrity. Satan's logic went along the lines of, "Sure, anybody who is as blessed as Job would follow You. But if he lost it all, would he remain faithful to You then?"

God granted Satan permission to test Job. "You can take everything," God said, "but don't lay a finger on him." Satan was ordered from the presence of God to do his worst.

The writer of the story then takes us back to the life of Job here on earth. What happens next will cause even the most confident of people to pause and think. Satan orchestrated one of the most horrific days for any man in recorded history. One day, when Job's children had gathered together at his oldest son's house for a feast, messengers began to arrive bearing terrible news. First, a messenger from Job's farming enterprise reported that had they been attacked, everything taken, and all the workers killed. As that messenger finished, another messenger from his shepherd industry reported that

Job's operation there has been hit by fire from the sky, which killed all his workers and flocks. Next, entered a messenger from his shipping and distribution company. Raiders had stolen all his camels, and all his workers were killed in the battle to protect the enterprise. And, finally, entered a messenger from the feast at his oldest son's house, saying that a mighty storm from the desert had blown in, destroying the house where Job's sons and daughters were and killing them all.

Job was overtaken with grief. But he did not deny God.

Our story cuts back to heaven. God questioned Satan about Job. Satan replied, "Sure, he hangs in there for now, but if You strike his body, he will begin to curse You." God gave Satan permission to attack Job's body, but not his life.

Satan was ordered from the presence of God. We cut back to Job.

Job's body was covered with painful sores, from the top of head to the soles of his feet. For relief, Job sat in ashes and scraped his sores with the sharp edges of broken pottery.

Satan started to play dirty, as he attempted a full-on attack on Job personally. Now the real testing began as Satan not only assaulted his body, but began an attack on Job's mind.

First his wife urged him to curse God and die. I believe Job's wife gets a bad rap here. Many describe her as a weak woman who lacked faith and turned on Job. I believe that her grief about her children was too much to bear. It was just the two of them dealing with their grief. I believe she had looked for comfort for her husband.

But now, Job was being afflicted. Her own pain she carried, along with seeing the pain of her husband, became too hard for her to withstand. She allowed her pain to convince her that death would be better than to continue in this existence they now find themselves in. I like Job's response to her:

> His wife said to him, "Are you still maintaining your integrity? Curse God and die!"

He replied, "You are talking like a foolish woman. Shall we accept good from God, and not trouble?"

In all this, Job did not sin in what he said.

Job 2:9,10

Note that Job said his wife was speaking *like* a foolish woman and not that she *was* a foolish woman. Job brought his wife back to their core belief that God would take care of them in times of prosperity and extreme hardship. Job's message was simple and powerful: God is in control; He knows, and He cares!

Satan weaponized Job's wife's love and grief to mount a psychological attack against him. After the loss of almost everything Satan piled on even more pressure. Would the physical and psychological attacks be the one-two punches that made Job turn his back on God?

Enter three well-intentioned critics of Job, disguised as friends. While they may have thought of themselves as well-meaning friends, Satan was about to use them to test Job and his beliefs.

Eliphaz, Bildad, and Zophar—I'll call them Eli, Bil, and Zo—had joined forces to comfort their friend in his grief. But they just couldn't help themselves, and they moved from giving sympathy to giving advice.

Eli and Bil took three shots each at giving their advice, while Zo gave his advice twice. I'm sure, as they surveyed the grief and destruction of Job, that they had placed themselves in his place. On the surface, their advice was condescending. By saying that Job must have sinned to cause these events in his life, they were setting themselves above Job. However, I think that maybe Satan had accused each of them. The thought that they could be next caused them internal grief. They may have thought that Job's problems could happen to anybody. If that was true, then there was a chance that this could happen to them, too. How could God be trusted? You'd better confess before even more hardship came your way.

I'm sure personal doubt and fear began to bubble to the surface in the three friends. That's probably why they sought solutions to prevent this from happening again . . . to them.

Job questioned his birth—did God make a mistake when He formed him? Job also questioned the story that God had placed him in. (Who wouldn't?) However, this opened the floodgate for his friends to give their opinions about Job's troubles.

The main questions that Job and his friends asked were these: "Where is wisdom to be found? What can we know about ourselves and God after events like this?" Job protested against God, citing his innocence and listing the principles he had lived by. He demanded a response from God. Eli declared that wisdom comes from dreams and visions. God gives blessings and is then declared to be God by the receivers.

God's answers came from a whirlwind. He did not defend His justice, and He did not answer directly Job's questions. Instead, God claimed His position as The Creator. He asked who helped God with the laying of the foundations of the world. Job's final response was one of retraction, repentance, and submission to the story that God had placed him in. Job received clarity. He once again saw the truth about himself.

But the story does not end there. Job was restored with children and grandchildren (and great-grandchildren and great-great-grandchildren!). His farming, shepherding, and distribution businesses were all restored and expanded beyond what they were before his calamity. Job went from pain, destruction, and criticism to loving his life and living his legacy.

Your critics will come. Even family and friends may turn on you. Why?

- Your failure is a comfort to them. Your victory would confront them with their lack of attention to the Dream the Creator has given them. If you withdraw from your

Dreamer's Quest, there will be an example of why they dare not embark upon their own Quest.

- Your testing raises fear within them. Your discomfort is too real for them as they watch you attempt to achieve your Dream. They may already know they must take on a Dreamer's Quest of their own. However, deep fear keeps them on the sidelines. Your confidence causes fear to rise within them. Their need to keep you from danger is a need to protect themselves from similar danger.

- There is a feeling of loss that fills their hearts. It could be loss of their Dream. It could be loss of you to your Dream, because they know they cannot travel with you. Or it could be loss of the vision they had for you.

- Your failure gives them a false sense of security. Maybe they tried and failed at their Dreamer's Quest a long time ago. They now paint the Quest as folly only for people who are "Dreamers". Predicting your failure, then seeing you fail, gives them a false sense of security in their ordinary lives.

- Your failure gives them a false sense of value. Predicting your failure gives them a false sense of value of themselves and their position. The Creator has never given anybody the Dream to be chief destroyer of Dreams. This person has a warped view that the Creator is all about punishment and destruction. By placing themselves in the role of judge, they have a false sense of who they are and what they have to offer. In a simple statement, they come to get and not to give.

To overcome these gatekeepers, you must counteract their claims with truth. If somebody comes to you with a legitimate claim that your actions are wrong, then you must consider the accusations and adjust your behavior if they're true. But you do not cave in or repent of your commitment to the Dream that God has given you. Your missteps in life don't mean an end to your Dream.

Here are some strategies to overcome Gatekeepers in your life:

- Listen with an open heart and mind, but be very protective of your Dream. Many times, I have needed to adjust my actions without losing my Dream. Remember, we are talking about *well-intentioned* critics. Sometimes they really do care about you and your Dream.

- Keep your focus on what you know to be true. Your identity, purpose, and meaning in life are gifts from God to you. You have a direct line to the Creator by way of your relationship with Jesus Christ. Make sure you keep the truth in sharp focus.

- Restrict the access negative people have to you. While you may need to have interactions with them, you must not allow a steady diet of negative input into your mind. Disciple your mind to focus on positive messages and images.

- Send out positive actions as much as possible. Pursue the good storyline within people you meet. Discover the good accomplishments of others, and repeat them to others. Be the CCO (Chief Cheerleading Officer) of your organization by always encouraging others. Catch others doing good. Encourage good, great, and excellent behavior. This has a way of repelling negative people and attracting positive people.

You will encounter Gatekeepers among your family and closest friends. They will tell you any number of ways that you will fail at pursuing your Dream. You will have to love them and encourage them upon the Dreamer's Quest. Make it a priority to serve them as much as possible. Love them as you want them to love you.

There will also be anonymous or distant critics. Glean from them as much as possible. Limit their access to you, but Love them all the same.

Keep the power of your Dream alive and protect it from harm. Your DNA has been clicked together for a purpose unique to you. You have been placed in your very own story to serve others. Once you understand these two life changing truths you will be able to better hear the voice of your creator. Jesus said, *"My sheep listen to my voice; I know them, and they follow me"* (John 10:27).

* * *

My stomach hurt after that confrontation with the parent over the cost of the youth conference. I sat stunned as I considered his words. I reviewed my motives.

I loved the students, and I wanted everybody to attend the conference. I had even been announcing for weeks that, if money was the only reason you were not signing up, to come see me and I would make sure you could attend. No, I wasn't gaining anything personally by charging more to cover the costs of the adult staff.

The interaction with this parent brought back a flood of memories of others who'd had harsh criticisms of me in the past. This wasn't the first time somebody had questioned my leadership.

- There was the time a couple of women accused me of gross doctrinal error when I introduced music with drums in the youth ministry.

- Or how about the time the man said I was encouraging lewd behavior by allowing students to handle microphones?

- Or the time the couple came in and said I was changing everything—and that I should take my music and games and leave town. (I've noticed, over the years, that music and games—anything from sports teams to mixers—can bring great drama and stress to churches. I think it is because, when we sing and play together, it is one of the few times when we are working together in unity. Makes sense to me that the enemy would attack here first.)

- Then there was the woman that was upset about how we handled snacks.

- Another "held me accountable" for my bad behavior at an event I didn't even attend.

All these well-intentioned critics had called for my removal and questioned my motives and character.

Now, there are the times when people called me on something I needed to hear. They pointed out a blind spot in my life that I needed to see. I have learned that I need to evaluate all criticism I receive. Just because somebody violated the command in the Bible to "speak the truth in love" does not mean their criticism was not worth consideration.

As I continued my self-reflection after the confrontation with the parent, I reviewed my Dream—my purpose for being at this church at this time. Why was I there? Had God designed me for this ministry at this time? Had God placed me in this church? Was I making a difference in teens and adult's lives? The answer was yes, on all counts.

As I reflected on the criticism, I gleaned a couple of truths that help guide me forward. I needed greater transparency in how we spent the funds that had been entrusted to us. I needed to make sure that volunteers, students, and parents felt love from me in the form of service. I needed to come across not as defensive, but as empowered to lead the youth ministry forward. I knew I needed to replace the negative words that were now seared into my brain with the words of my calling. I needed to make those words more real than the words of negativity.

I waged this war internally for several months. It was a war for my emotions, my heart, my soul, my spirit—and it became a battle for my body. The anxiety I felt caused stress, loss of sleep, and a mild depression. Even to recount the story here brings back that same anxiety I experienced those many years ago. I am fighting the same battles all over again, even though I have won victory before. There is still a need to knock down the flames again and again.

That is the nature of this battle. It will hit you from close in, using family and friends to take your focus away from your Dreamer's Quest. Even seeing an image or hearing a song can transport you back to the Dare Gate again, to wage war with the same enemy.

After you have mined the truth that will help you move forward in your Dreamer's Quest, you must discipline your mind.

Finally, brothers and sisters, whatever is true, whatever is noble, whatever is right, whatever is pure, whatever is lovely, whatever is admirable—if anything is excellent or praiseworthy—think about such things.

Philippians 4:8

The discipline of being the gatekeeper of your mind will allow you to properly defend yourself from external gatekeepers who try to bully their way into your life. You may never be able to determine if these gatekeepers are well-intentioned, or if they mean you harm.

The truth is sometimes difficult to determine when you are attacked from the blind side (whether by those close to you, or from people you know from afar). You must guard your heart and mind, making it a priority to remain connected to what you know to be true. You do this by actively connecting to what you know by asking yourself some key questions: Are you fixing my thoughts on what is true, noble, pure, and right about your actions and motives?

Can you list what is lovely and admirable in your life? You must become proactive when dealing with these critics. If you remain passive, you will open yourself to suggestion. This will nearly always lead you astray from your desired goals. Are there some actions you can take to better discipline your mind when you are facing challenges?

If you are having trouble compiling a list of lovely and admirable thoughts in your mind, replace the ideas that come into your mind with new, positive contributions.

If your mind dwells upon thoughts that are not admirable, excellent, and praiseworthy, meditate upon ideas, contributions, responses, and feedback that are.

Monitoring your input will maximize your output of right thinking.

Vigilance of thought will bring confidence of action. You are in a battle for your mind. *For as he thinks within himself, so he is . . .*

Proverbs 23:7a New American Standard Bible

* * *

THE DREAMER'S JOURNAL

Tony Robbins, a motivational speaker, author, and entrepreneur, was born in North Hollywood, California in 1960. He is the oldest of three children. He was adopted by Jim Robbins, a semi-professional baseball player, at the age of twelve. His mother had, as he puts it, "a series of husbands." He was raised in Glendora, California and attended high school there. He describes his life as "chaotic" and "abusive," which led to him leaving home at age seventeen, to never return. He worked as a janitor and did not attend college.

It was at the age of seventeen that he joined the organization of Jim Rohn, a thought leader and speaker. Tony learned how to promote seminars from Jim, who became a mentor to him. He taught Tony how to think and which subjects to think about.

Today, Tony is the author of five bestsellers. He has spoken to over 4 million people and has coached some of the most famous people in the world, such as Wayne Gretzky, Serena Williams, Pitbull, and even Bill Clinton. He has part ownership in the Los Angeles Football Club (pro soccer), Team Liquid, an esports pro gaming organization, and a beautiful resort in the Fiji Islands. He is now ranked 62 on Forbes' wealth power rankings, at $480 million net worth.

With ownership in over 30 companies that operate in more than 100 countries, he has become the poster child for the rags-to-riches club. Even after giving all the proceeds from his book sales to feed the hungry, he still manages to turn a profit with speaking appearances related to his books. He commands as much as $300,000 for one speech, and can sell out seminars to 2,000 people at $10,000 per participant. He has done so for many years now—yet he is still not 60 years old! He is on track to become a member of the billionaire club in the next five to seven years.

How could a janitor with no formal education make such a huge move in his life? Tony understands the need and the power of preparing his mind. By keeping his mind, spirit, and body pure, he remains focused on his Dream. Performing daily morning rituals to cleanse his mind, body, and spirit, he is the gatekeeper of his heart and soul.

He prepares his mind every day with reading. He keeps only positive thoughts pouring into his mind. He also does a morning routine of exercise, which includes a cold plunge into 57-degree water. His diet is very strict and healthy as well. By becoming a lifelong learner, he has eliminated the need to spend years in college and university to achieve his Dream: to aid others in overcoming the limits they face.

8

DELETING YOUR SCRIPTS: THE FALSE SCRIPTS WE BELIEVE

Whether you think you can, or think you can't, you're right.

Henry Ford

* * *

Have you ever realized that you are talking to yourself? I do all the time! My awareness of this ongoing conversation comes in a flash. And when I stop to really think about it, I realize the conversation has been going on for a very long time. Some of us let this internal exchange of ideas slip into the external world. I catch my wife, Sandy, having full conversations with herself. I sometimes wonder who wins those arguments.

You may mutter to yourself. You may go into a dark room all alone and let a stream of words that express hidden feelings escape from your inner being. You may bottle up all this conversation deep within your mind—you consider it "thinking," a much less emotional expression than "talking to yourself." Or, you may be aware of this internal talk within your soul.

Your awareness of these conversations is vitally important. Without an internal gatekeeper, you let outside forces influence your conversations with yourself. While this can be a good influence, it is just as likely that it will be negative.

I didn't understand my self-talk as a boy. I just thought it was words that bounced around my head. I didn't understand the value or the harm those little words could bring my way. Being raised like an only child (remember, my older brothers were in their teens when I was born), I only understood that when I was lonely, I could count on these conversations to keep me company.

Many years into my adult life, I began to decode those conversation with myself. What had I said to myself as a boy, and why had I said it? I began to mine the various topics that I told myself, even though I could not remember the conversations themselves. Three major themes surfaced. They were not positive, and I had to confront them head on.

- My sense of acceptance: *Nobody wants me around. I'm just in the way.*

- My sense of my inner being: *I'm ugly, dumb and stupid. I don't have any talent, and I will never have anything to offer.*

- My sense of my worth and value: *I'm a loser. A disappointment to everyone around me.*

As an adult, these words conflicted with other words that floated around my head. I couldn't understand how to reconcile these competing viewpoints.

- My sense of purpose: *I will be part of a winning team. I will make a difference in others' lives. I will leave my mark on the world.*

- My sense of my identity: *I have talents that are important. I have insights that others don't have. I understand matters in ways others don't and that is a great assistance to those around me.*

- My sense of my value: *I will make a difference in people's lives one day.*

It was like in the old cartoons that ran on TV in my childhood. There was a devil sitting on one shoulder telling me I was not wanted, no good, and a loser. But then, in a flash, the little angel would appear on my other shoulder, telling me I was an important person, smart and intelligent, and I was going to win at life.

This internal conflict could make me think just maybe I was a bit crazy. *Why do I have these competing voices in my mind, and which one should I listen to?* I thought. I began to compile evidence to prove which of these voices was true. My negative side had more data. Take for example my self-limiting belief that nobody wanted me around.

My mother was thrust into caring for her younger brothers and sisters when she was a teen, after her mother died from cancer. She married my dad when she was seventeen years old, moved to Florida to wait for his discharge from the Navy, and then moved back to Tennessee. Back on the farm, she had two children and she worked in the munitions factory. Then, after moving to Pontiac, she had a tubal pregnancy (resulting in a miscarriage) and was told she would never have children again. Then I showed up, the "miracle child."

But I never felt like a miracle child. I felt more like an intruder. I saw myself as an extra burden on top of the hardship my family had suffered. I was too young to understand all these feelings, but the roots had been already planted in my heart.

Around the age of six or seven, I had a life-shattering conversation with my mom. I'm not sure about everything that was going with her during this period in her life, but I do remember the conversation. I was in trouble for something I had done. She told me that my nickname was "Boo-Boo" not because of Boo-Boo Bear in *The Yogi Bear Show*, but because I was a boo-boo—a mistake. I wasn't supposed to be there. She had hoped for a little girl, and I was such a disappointment to her.

I had all the evidence I needed. Nobody wanted me around. The other voice was just a lie or my pride talking to me. I was not smart, and I would never amount to anything. I became very shy, and I withdrew within myself. I especially had issues around girls and women. I didn't know why. I wanted to be accepted, but I felt I would never gain a sense of belonging. It was easier to believe the lies about myself.

Later, in my college years, I crystallized these feelings into a mantra: "Who knows, who cares, why try?" When others asked how my prep was going for a paper or an exam, my answer would be received with laughs or strange looks. For some reason, I could never silence the other voice that contradicted the negative feeling I had about myself. *I must be crazy!* I thought. *How can I feel I'm not wanted and had nothing to offer, but also feel I'm going to win, make a difference, and be part of a winning team?*

* * *

TRANSFORMATION OF IDENTITY: WHAT IS THE REAL SCRIPT FOR MY LIFE?

A boy named Saul was born around AD 5 in the city of Tarsus. (In antiquity, Tarsus was in the southern coastal region of Asia Minor known as Cilicia. Tarsus is in modern day Turkey.) However, during most of his youth, he and his family lived together in Jerusalem. Saul's parents had the distinction of being both Jewish and Roman citizens. This heritage and its privileges were passed on to Saul as birthrights. They would open opportunities for education that would become important during his adult life.

Sometime between AD 15 and AD 20, Saul began his studies of the Hebrew Scriptures in Jerusalem. It was during this time that the famous Rabbi Gamaliel was taking students, and young Saul had the great distinction to became one. It was considered an honor to be one of the chosen few taught by this scholar of the Hebrew law.

Under Rabbi Gamaliel, Saul became an expert in the Hebrew law and entered the sect known as the Pharisees. In the time of Jesus, much like our political parties today, the Pharisees and Sadducees were the two main "parties" that made up the Jewish ruling body called the Sanhedrin.

Saul took on the role of defender of the Jewish faith as a young man. Saul ravaged the early Christian church by arresting both men and women believers. He was also present at the death of Stephen, the first martyr of the Christian faith. Those who carried out the execution of Stephen placed their coats at the feet of Saul, who gave full approval of their actions. It could be that Saul's status as Pharisee kept him from throwing the stones, but gave him the authority to order the mob's actions.

The transformation of Saul—the persecutor of Christianity—to becoming Paul—the writer of most of the New Testament, ardent missionary to the unbelieving world, and servant in the face of personal persecutions—is beyond extraordinary. Just the story of his conversion is special (Acts 9:3-9). As he was in route to Damascus for another round of persecution, a bright light appeared in the sky, and the voice of Jesus confronted him. Saul was blinded and led into the city. There he met with one of the Christian leaders he was going to imprison, to learn how to become a follower of Jesus Christ.

Ananias had serious questions about meeting the man sent to kill Christians. But Ananias was sent by God to guide Saul into a personal relationship with Jesus Christ. The transformation from Saul to Paul took place. While the transformation happened in an instant, it took years of re-learning his beliefs for Paul to truly step into his Dream—to be the defender of truth. God had clicked his DNA together in just the right way and placed him within the right story so Paul could pursue his real Dream within. A few years later, he emerged as one of the most important personalities within the Christian faith: the author of most of the New Testament.

The words of this former persecutor of Christians are so important for us today. His words give us hope that we, too, can be transformed from our out dated, false script. Paul's message of transformation in Romans 12:1-2 still has massive meaning for us today:

> *Therefore, I urge you, brothers and sisters, in view of God's mercy, to offer your bodies as a living sacrifice, holy and pleasing to God—this is your true and proper worship. Do not conform to the pattern of this world but be transformed by the renewing of your mind. Then you will be able to test and approve what God's will is—his good, pleasing and perfect will.*

Paul has just taken the first eleven chapters to explain the details of Salvation through faith, a personal relationship with Jesus Christ. He has explained why salvation comes through the Children of Israel, why we have such a hard time living in relationship with Jesus, and how the record books are set straight so there is no debt or guilt in our becoming members of the family of God.

There is so much meaningful detail about a personal relationship with God in the first eleven chapters of the book of Romans that it has spawned the writing of millions of sermons, talks, lectures, and books. It is one of the foundational works of Christianity.

Then, in Chapter 12, Paul takes a pivot into a deeper question. How does all this matter in the daily lives of followers of Jesus Christ? He answers the question we all have, but are afraid to say out loud: *So what?!* What difference does this make to me?

Let's take a closer look at the beliefs that result in transformation.

- Belief that reveals you are designed for greatness and to win! *"Therefore, I urge you, brothers and sisters, in view of God's mercy . . ."* God's mercy is the starting point of transformation. You cannot stray so far out of bounds that you reach a place beyond God's mercy. You may not understand the love behind God's mercy, but it's there for you to accept. The foundation of transformation is not found inside of you, but within a relationship with the Creator who placed the Dream within you. When you make that all-in commitment to Him, at that moment, you begin to move from Ordinary to Extraordinary.

- Belief that results in your total commitment to the Dream! *". . . to offer your bodies as a living sacrifice, holy and pleasing to God—this is your true and proper worship."* Total commitment means giving yourself totally to the Dream. To be totally committed is to see yourself as a worthy living sacrifice, not because of who you think you are, but because of your personal relationship with the Creator. You throw yourself into the plans the Creator has designed for you.

- Belief that changes your understanding of the blueprints for your life! *Do not conform to the pattern of this world . . ."* If you continue to conform to the pattern of this world, you will continue to be imprisoned in Ordinary. You must replace all your former patterns of thinking with new patterns. This will appear radical to the outside observer, who has never been part of a Dreamer's Quest. They only know the land of Ordinary and its values. Most times, the values of Extraordinary are in the opposite direction of the model the people of Ordinary follow.

- Belief that radicalizes your approach to the Dream! *". . . but be transformed by the renewing of your mind."* You have been created for greatness. You have been designed to win! Living your legacy has everything to do with the transformation of your mind. It is important to note that this is a "renewal" of your mind. This is the rediscovery of the original design the Creator had in mind for you. The wrong choices you have made, the false beliefs you have assumed, and the pressure of this world's pattern have marred the hidden beauty of the Creator's design for you. You need a renewal of your mind (the beliefs that drive your actions) to recapture your personal Dream given to you by the Creator.

- Belief that results in understanding and clarity of the Dream! *"Then you will be able to test and approve what God's will is—his good, pleasing and perfect will."* A test is a procedure to establish the validity of a belief or idea. It can also be an event or situation that reveals the strength of a concept or philosophy. In Malachi 3:10, we find God speaking to Israel, challenging them to do something counterintuitive:

> *"Bring the whole tithe into the storehouse, that there may be food in my house. Test me in this," says the LORD Almighty, "and see if I will not throw open the floodgates of heaven and pour out so much blessing that there will not be room enough to store it."*
>
> Malachi 3:10

Note that God is not averse to the challenge of a test. You show your worship by offering you bodies as living sacrifices, not conforming to the pattern of this world, transforming you mind, giving the first 10 percent of your harvest, or Awakening to the Dreamer's Quest— and see if the Creator doesn't bless you beyond what you could ever imagine. This is where you put your beliefs to the test.

This is amazing news. God knows you personally: in fact, He has designed you and placed you into this life for greatness and to win! The bad news is that we all enter this world by way of Ordinary. We make choices that separate us from having a relationship with the Creator. We choose to follow a path that leads us away from the Creator. Even though you have taken the wrong path, made bad choices, listened to false beliefs, and followed the storyline the world around you has fed you, God is still waiting for you to test Him in all of this.

For it is with your heart that you believe and are justified, and it is with your mouth that you profess your faith and are saved.

Romans 10:10

The word "justified" here is an accounting term. It means your accounts have been settled. All the false beliefs that have led on wayward excursions are a result of following the belief system of Ordinary. You have created a debt because of your rebellion against the Creator's design for you. However, all your debts are settled, and all the injury to your relationship with the Creator is forgiven. This occurs when you trust in Jesus Christ, the Creator, and you proclaim that belief with your mouth. It is at this point when you Observe—see, believe, and conform the Creator's design for your life—and you become justified. This is the true Awakening. Some call it being "born again," and others simply say, "Jesus saved me."

This is true only because Jesus, the Creator, followed the plan the Godhead placed into motion before the foundation of the world. The Trinity went all-in for you by sending the Son, Jesus, to the world where he became a man, living to perfection the Dream placed before him.

Jesus then finished that plan by paying our debt though His death on the cross for each of us. Knowing you would fail to live by the Creator's design, He made a path for you to enter a relationship with Him. All we must do is believe and receive the gift of Awakening. Along with this gift comes the opportunity to pursue the original purpose for our lives. We are now able to recapture that original design for our lives. You are on the Quest to find the real meaning of your life.

It is now up to you as to how much you will decide to Believe. *Awakening! The Dreamer's Quest* is based upon the foundational trues that the universe operates upon:

- Belief that reveals you are designed for greatness!

- Belief that resolves your total commitment to the Dream!

- Belief that radicalizes your approach to the Dream!

- Belief that results in understanding of the Dream!

Self-limiting beliefs cannot withstand the enduring power of a transformed mind. Transformation of your mind is the first and most important step to flipping the script. This radical belief system has the potential to destroy negative self-talk. Now you must apply it.

Because of his standing in the ruling body of the Jewish people, Paul must have heard the claims that Jesus Christ was the messiah. He listened to the leaders of this ruling body denounce the claims. He probably not only listened to the arguments, but denounced the message himself. Being present at the execution of Stephen, Paul would have heard Stephen's last words of faith in Jesus and seen that belief put into action. He would have heard the testimony of the followers of Jesus as he imprisoned them. Then, to have Jesus confront him supernaturally was life-transforming.

Paul became a leader within the Christian community he had once persecuted. He accepted the script that God had written for him before creation, to take the gospel to the Gentiles, the non-Jewish communities that had oppressed Israel. The same communities he was taught to shun.

Paul's transformation was a total departure from what he had planned for himself (and what others had planned for him). But it was the exact path that the Creator had designed him for. The world was waiting for him to become the intellectual leader of the Christian faith.

Paul was transformed. This set him on a path of his Dreamer's Quest that would lead him to preach to the most powerful audiences of his time. He saw his message received and rejected by members of the household of Caesar. After his death, others took his message of transformation, and his writings about that transformation, to become the foundation for a worldwide movement.

The truth of the matter is that Paul simply believed the story of Jesus Christ. This transformed him from being a persecutor of that message to being empowered to pursue his Dream: the defender of Truth. Just like Jesus Christ, Paul's mission was to serve and not to be served. This is the model for each of us. To have the Awakening within our souls. To pursue the Dreamer's Quest set before us. To serve others with our newfound mission. All of this begins with the transformation of your mind, which leads to actions, which lead to habits, which lead us to our legacy.

Now that you have experienced a transformed mind, you will need to strengthen it— demolishing the tests, trials, and obstacles to your Dreamer's Quest, which we will look at in the next chapter.

* * *

Although I had overcome the voices within my head that said I was ugly, dumb and unwanted many times before, they were back again. This time, it came just after I had made the transition into being on my own, starting a ministry in Florida. If you remember, the stock market had crashed, and my startup non-profit had little hope of surviving. Thoughts of my stupidity, inadequacies, and failures crowded out the Dream. Nobody wanted me in Orlando. These thoughts consumed me, and I had plenty of evidence that they were true.

I was in need of radical reconditioning of my mind. I knew I needed to change my thinking, but how? I had to retrace my steps. Where did I get derailed from my Dream?

I finally got all the way back to my Awakening. It was the moment I discovered again that my Dream was not dependent upon me, but upon my story. I began to connect again with this positive message of the Gospel: God has a plan for me! Not to harm me, but to make me successful.

This led me to recommit to the pursuit of the Dream within. Doing this created even more positive thoughts: not only could this happen, but it was going to happen. My faith was strengthened, and the negative voices began to quiet down.

If you have ever been to the ocean, you know that the water line does not remain constant. At times, you will have a lot of beach to walk on. Then there are times that the water creeps up onto the beach, covering most of what was visible a few hours ago. An experienced beachgoer will know the high-water line, and set up their spot above the high tide mark.

Inexperienced beachgoers will invariably set up their beach equipment close to the water's edge so they can be close to the action of the waves. A few hours later, to their utter surprise, the beach has moved beneath them—or, might I say, the ocean has moved. The tide has turned. The waterline is no longer moving out to sea, but has started to creep its way back toward dry land.

Experienced beachgoers watch with knowing smiles as the surprised newbies frantically snatch their things and drag them to safety. It's really entertaining when they don't move far enough up the beach, and repeat the scene one or two more times.

There is a tide in our thought lives. An ebb and flow from the negative thought patterns to the positive thought patterns. Some set up in that narrow margins of safety, where the negative thought patterns of Ordinary cannot creep up on them. Others, wanting to be as close to the action as possible, set up at water's edge. They are surprised when everything they have is caught under the tide of negative thoughts. Frantically, they try to deal with the approaching doom. Their reactions may vary:

- They may stand in disbelief, watching everything they own become immersed in the rising tide.

- Some run up the beach, leaving everything behind to the mercy of the incoming waves.

- Others will blame it on the ocean or on the people who took up the better spots.

- Some will just scoop belongings onto their laps—sitting in their beach chairs, playfully waving their feet in the waves, acting like they meant to do this all along. They are becoming engulfed in the waves around them, but it's not an issue. Just another day at the beach.

- Some won't understand why there is a problem. They set up here yesterday in the same spot, and everything was fine!

Part of renewing your mind is being proactive about what you allow into your mind. Where you set up your beach chair will determine your experience at the beach. What you allow your mind to dwell on will determine your experience in life. For all of us, we first set up too close to the water's edge. We need to make a move—have a transformation. The Creator has set you up with a beautiful cabana, equipped just for you. You may think it is restrictive, or that it will cost you too much to stay in your cabana, but it's the place designed just for you.

I have experienced thrills beyond description in my Dreamer's Quest. All of them have come from following the Apostle Paul's formula of transformation. A moment when you realize you are designed by the Creator for greatness that leads to a decisive moment of total commitment to this course that leads to even greater clarity of your Dream!

I used to tell myself that the cabanas are for rich people, for special people who deserve the best treatment. Recently, our family had the opportunity to use a cabana. The experience was transforming. I never want to go back to sitting in the sand and the sun. I thought I hated the beach—not true. I hated the fight with the ocean and the sand.

When you experience a transformation in your thinking, you will see the world in a whole new light. What you thought you hated may become enjoyable. What you thought was normal will no longer be normal. And what you thought was reserved for only the elite may become your New Ordinary.

* * *

THE DREAMER'S JOURNAL

On the Mayo Clinic website, there is an informative article about negative self-talk.[2] It points out that positive thinking is not the absence of anything negative in your life. It is also not denying that things go wrong. It is your interpretation of events in your life. How you write your story in your mind is very important.

There is a stream of thought running through your mind all day long. You may not even be aware of it, but it is there. What you are saying to yourself has a profound effect on what you believe about yourself and the world you live in. The article lists the health benefits of positive thinking:

- Increased life span

- Lower rates of depression

- Lower levels of distress

- Greater resistance to the common cold

- Better psychological and physical well-being

- Better cardiovascular health and reduced risk of death from cardiovascular disease

- Better coping skills during hardships and times of stress

What was your interpretation of that list? That you may live a longer life, or a shorter life? That you will be depressed, or that you will overcome depression? Did you think you would have distress, or colds, or psychological, physical, or

---

[2]   "Positive Thinking: Stop Negative Self-Talk to Reduce Stress." Mayo Clinic. February 18, 2017. https://www.mayoclinic.org/healthy-lifestyle/stress-management/in-depth/positive-thinking/art-20043950).

cardiovascular diseases? Did you feel you could cope better or worse with hardships and stress?

Your interpretation of the message is very important.

There is still a little boy inside of me, sitting under the maple tree in the backyard and listening to the voices in my mind. If I leave myself unchecked, I go back to the patterns that were set deep within my heart all those years ago. I have worn ruts that are deep and smooth, carved into my heart. It is easy to go to autopilot, allowing negative thoughts to silence the calling that my purpose gives me today.

I must purposefully determine the path I will take in life. I must take steps to make it the pattern for my life. It takes determination and confidence to achieve the desired goals for my life. It also takes some skill to master with confidence the positive traits I had as a boy, and to silence the negative thoughts that bounce off the walls of my mind.

Here are some strategies I have learned to use in the transformation of my mind. You can use these ideas to protect the transformation of your mind from the negative self-beliefs you face:

Check yourself and *identify areas of opportunity for growth in your thinking.* Roger Hall, Ph. D. of Compass Consultation Ltd. is an executive coach. In his book "Expedition" he gives a method of testing your stream of consciousness. That is the continual stream of conversation you are having with yourself at this very moment. He recommends that you set your smart phone alarm to go off once every hour, ten hours per day, for seven days. When the alarm sounds, you record what you are thinking. If it is "I want a cheeseburger" you record that. If it is "I'm tired" or "I'm upset" you record that. At the end of the week you will have 70 audits of your thoughts. This will show you the areas you need to work on first. It will also help you develop the habit of self-auditing your thoughts moving forward. You will be able to slow down your thinking, catch your thoughts, and adjust them.

Be healthy. Maintaining proper health is very important to your thought processes. Enough rest, proper fuel for your body, regular exercise routine, time spent with loved ones, expanding your mind with positive new ideas, and finally, connecting with your Creator spiritually every day—these will all provide a foundation for positive self-talk. This will require a disciple that you maintain around your heart.

Guard your heart. Be vigilant with the gate to your heart. Allow in only those who provide positive input to your life. Understanding the truth is very important for a positive mental health. Denial of your situation can be even more destructive than negative self-beliefs.

> *Above all else, guard your heart,*
> *for everything you do flows from it.*

> Proverbs 4:23

Take precautions to have positive people in your life. Make sure you have positive, supportive people in your life. Seek this circle of positive influence for advice.

Be Positive. Make sure you speak to yourself in a positive, wholesome fashion. The Creator has commanded us to "love your neighbor." But that is only part of the quote of the command given to us. The full text of this command is:

> *Jesus replied: "Love the Lord your God with all your heart and with all your soul and with all your mind. This is the first and greatest commandment. And the second is like it: 'Love your neighbor as yourself.'"*

> Matthew 22:37-39

First, notice that love is more than just a matter of the heart and soul, but also of the mind. Next, notice that you are to love your neighbor as yourself. It is implied here that you must love yourself in a healthy manner (with heart, soul, and mind). The foundation of our service to the world is a healthy love of ourselves. Self-loathing is not helpful for anybody concerned.

Discipline your mind to think about positive things. It will take work to build healthy habits in your thought life. What you say to yourself today, you will reap tomorrow. We will refer to this passage several times:

> *Finally, brothers and sisters, whatever is true, whatever is noble, whatever is right, whatever is pure, whatever is lovely, whatever is admirable—if anything is excellent or praiseworthy—think about such things.*
>
> Philippians 4:8

It will take effort, work, and discipline to place your mind on the right things. But the freedom from negative self-beliefs is priceless.

9

DARE TO DIMINISH DETOURS: PERCEIVING YOUR PROBLEMS AS BLESSINGS IN DISGUISE

All the adversity I've had in my life, all my troubles and obstacles, have strengthened me [...] You may not realize it when it happens, but a kick in the teeth may be the best thing in the world for you.

Walt Disney

* * *

It all started in August 2015 with Sandy's trip to the doctor for what we thought was a chest infection. That trip led to an ambulance ride to the ER, and to the first-ever hospital stay in her life. We learned that Sandy (my wife, in case you don't remember) had Atrial Fibrillation (Afib) and Atrial Flutter (Aflutter). These are common issues.

Afib occurs when your heart has a quivery, fluttery heartbeat. You might have heard it called "arrhythmia." It can lead to poor blood flow or heart failure. It can also allow blood to pool inside your heart and form clots. If one of these clots gets stuck in your brain, you could have a stroke. Aflutter is the same issue, but originates from a different chamber of the heart.

Both run the same risks, and many times, like Sandy, a patient will jump back and forth between these two rhythms. However, Sandy stood in a class all her own. She had no symptoms to alert her of these heart troubles, and she was not able to feel anything out of the ordinary. To add to the confusion, the prescribed medications were not keeping her heart in regular rhythm. We tracked her heart rate for weeks on end, and it never dropped below 150 beats per minute. Over the next three years she would receive four ablations to try and stop these rhythms from reoccurring and twelve or thirteen cardioversions to shock her heart back into normal rhythm.

It was October 28, 2018 when we had made our way to the hospital for her fourth ablation, in hopes to curing the abnormal electrical activity that was causing the problems in her heart. This time the pre-op procedures felt different, and Sandy was feeling anxious about the procedure. Her anxiety heightened as seven nurses and doctors descended upon her, working to prep the surgical areas and connect IVs and monitors. All the activity was different from our previous hospital experiences and was a bit frightening to both of us.

I prayed with her, reassured her that the doctors would take good care of her, and gave her a kiss just before the nurses and doctors took her to surgery. The doctors assured me they would take good care of her, and they left with urgency. I felt a little uneasy, but I had been through this several times before, so I tried to shake off the feelings.

I retreated to the surgical waiting area, just down the hall from the operating room. As I tried to busy myself with social media on my phone, I heard a call over the public address system. It sounded out a "code blue" in the surgical unit on the floor where Sandy was being operated upon. Being a viewer of medical shows on TV, I knew this was *not* a code you wanted to hear while your wife was in surgery. It was early in the morning, and I had not seen any other families waiting for their family members. Could that be Sandy? I tried not to let my imagination run wild. I said yet another prayer for her and the doctors in charge of her care. About ten minutes later, there was another announcement canceling the "code blue" in the surgical ward, on the same floor they had just called out.

Once again, my mind raced. I reviewed all the hospital shows I had watched over the years, trying to decipher what this all meant. I said more prayers. Then my daughter walked in. We chatted a bit as I caught her up on the events of the morning, leaving out the "code blue" calls. I didn't want to worry her, and I didn't want my mind dwelling upon all kinds of fantasies of what could be happening down the hall.

The procedure was to take three to four hours. About an hour and a half into it, out walked our cardio surgeon. He looked bad—almost defeated. He said that Sandy was in recovery and that she was doing great. However, he explained, when the doctors placed her under anesthesia, her heart rate jumped to 220 beats per minute. Her blood pressure dropped so low that it didn't register. When they checked her for a pulse, they could not find one. They had to perform a cardioversion to place her back into sinus rhythm. However, they were not able to do the procedure they had planned on because she had converted back to sinus rhythm (she was back in normal heart rhythm).

It was later during Sandy's stay in the hospital that I was able to place all the pieces of the puzzle together. The code blue was for Sandy. Her heart rate was very high while she was being prepped for surgery. When the doctors administered the anesthesia, her heart went into an even higher heart rate that did not pump any blood. They were not able to get a pulse. She was in serious trouble. God had been watching over her and the doctors. It was just one more test of our faith. But

127

it was the beginning of yet another test. We were introduced to a new cardio surgeon and a new procedure. This time, the surgeons would be attempting a new procedure that was more aggressive and riskier. But there was a 70 to 80 percent chance for a complete cure.

It would be a full week until the next attempt. While we waited in the hospital, they placed her on new drugs to get her heart rate under control, and they would not let her out of bed for more than bathroom breaks. We spent a lot of time together. Time in prayer. Time just sitting together with the TV on. Time spent with our daughters.

The day came for surgery. I was allowed to see Sandy just before the procedure. She was already hooked up to just about every device you could think of. The effects of anesthesia were already setting in as we prayed yet again. Then Sandy decided she wanted to spend these last moments quoting Bible verses. She quoted a verse that had an "A" word in it. Then "B" . . . and so we went through the entire alphabet. Most of the verses were a huge encouragement to me. I later found out that Sandy does not remember doing this at all.

This surgery was much longer than any of the others. It started around noon, and it was after six when we finally spoke with her doctor. He used words like "cured" and "great." I was starting to feel like things would get better.

That is, until I entered the ICU to see Sandy. She was still asleep and on the breathing machine (I guess its proper name is a ventilator). She looked pretty bad. Memories came flooding back of being with loved ones in their final moments. I was afraid! I felt a deep dread that Sandy was leaving me. While I knew that she would be in a better place, it just couldn't be her time to depart for glory—could it?

Although my daughters were right there beside me, this time I prayed alone. I felt alone. I felt my faith being tossed in a sea of doubts and regrets.

I'd had the same feelings just a few months before, when I was the one going in for heart surgery. I had a blocked artery. It was the fourth surgery I had undergone in a year to open the blockage. I felt vulnerable. I wondered if I would wake up from this dream. My faith was being tested again.

Sandy had asked me in our week together before this surgery about being afraid. She wanted to know if I was facing the same fears she was experiencing. We had the same feelings. I had to stay the course, but the fear was real. I only had the idea of standing firm to encourage both of us to remain faithful.

As I walked away from that scary visit with my wife, I said to myself, *"Consider it pure joy?" Jesus, you are going to have to help me with that one.*

* * *

Jesus had a younger brother named James. Can you imagine Joseph and Mary's home life? Your firstborn is the Son of God. Perfect in every way. You think you are a great parent, so you have a couple more kids. But there is something very different about the next kids. They are not perfect.

Consider what it must have been like for James, the younger brother of Jesus. Jesus was perfect; James was not. Other than the missing child report when he got separated from the family at Passover, Jesus had a clean record. Even this incident took a turn for the good when he was found three days later, teaching in the temple courts. He had found a place among the teachers there, listening and asking questions. Everybody was impressed with his understanding of scriptures.

When his parent found him, they were "astonished," the scripture says. Mary, overtaken with fear that she had misplaced the Son of God, must have grabbed him like a good Jewish mother, crying from fear, grief, and happiness all at the same time. Sounding like any other mother, she said, "Son, why have you treated us like this? Your father and I have been anxiously searching for you."

Even when you thought Jesus was going to really get it, he said to them, "Why were you searching for me? Didn't you know I had to be in my Father's house?" Not really understanding what he was saying, they gathered him up and return home.

I believe that this story was told repeatedly. His family, including his brothers and sisters, must have revisited this moment. Many other stories probably stood out in their minds as being odd, too. I'm sure James had his fill of being compared to Jesus.

James' life was surely filled with moments when he didn't understand where his older brother was coming from. It was only after Jesus rose in popularity and infamy, and was betrayed, crucified, buried, and raised from the dead, that this changed. He became convicted that Jesus was more than just his brother, and James became a disciple of Jesus.

James quickly became a leader in the church of Jerusalem, which came under persecution shortly after Jesus' ascension into heaven. This persecution sent many of the believers escaping to remote places far away from Jerusalem. It was in this environment of fear that James, who was now the leader of the church of Jerusalem, wrote a letter to the church. His Jewish congregation of believers in Jerusalem was being persecuted. God used this persecution to spread the Gospel, as members of the Jerusalem church fled for safety to other cities and regions. James wrote a letter to encourage his scattered congregation. We know that letter as the Book of James.

James' life had been filled with obstacles, setbacks, well-intentioned gatekeepers, and a whole host of fears and doubts. I'm sure he had the same issues we all face. Was he enough? Did he have enough leadership to step into the identity God had designed for him? The scattered members of his church needed leadership from someone who understood their situation. James was just the man.

He jumped right into their painful situation by giving them perspective. He did not look for somebody to blame. He gave no excuses. He did not deny their pain. He imparted to them some perspective about trials, testing, and temptations. We all can use this same perspective to help us face the fears, doubts, obstacles, and well-intentioned critics we all have.

TRIALS—IN THIS LIFE YOU WILL HAVE TROUBLES!

Life is hard! Everybody knows that. But it is not a randomly hard life. It is hard with a purpose. The "hard" in life reveals the Divine design hidden within each of us. It also reveals how short we fall of that hidden design. Remember, we are the product of the Creator, who had a very specific purpose in mind for each person He created. He has plans for you—and those plans are not meant to harm you, but to prosper you.

However, there is absolutely no evidence that our lives will suddenly get easy after we embark upon the Dreamer's Quest. The idea that the trials will stop coming our way if we do this or that is false. In fact, I believe the Creator has sent us the message that the more we can handle, the more will come our way. It is in this setting that James begins his letter, with these words:

"Consider it pure joy, my brothers, whenever you face trails of many kinds."

James 1:2

As hard as it is to believe, the trials that we normally label as "bad" really are the events that carve greatness into our lives.

Consider the process of learning any new skill. When you first set out, you are terrible. You look awkward. You may even make others uneasy as they watch your attempts to implement the new skill into your life. As a youth pastor, I have had my

131

moments of anxiety as I've watched teens attempt skills like singing, speaking, or leading. Being given the opportunity to try can be painful but necessary to attempt to accomplish new skills.

I remember trying to learn how to shoot a basketball. Oh, man, those are some painful memories. Launching a ball precisely enough to go through a hoop suspended ten feet in the air was beyond my comprehension as a young boy. I would watch players on the playground shoot. They made it look easy. When I attempted to make the shot, many times I would miss everything. Or as we used to say: "I didn't draw iron," "I laid a brick," or the famous, "Air ball!"

These repeated attempts would only deepen my love for the game. I would spend hours shooting, only to run down the errant shot to try again and again. Slowly I learned proper technique, and my muscles strengthened.

This process took years. It was hard. It was discouraging. It was worth it. I loved playing basketball. I loved being part of a team that worked together to score points and to defend our goal. Shooting was just one of many skills I had to master to be part of the team. It was hard, but it brought such joy.

I never outgrew the need to learn more skills. It was hard to keep learning and practicing. Practice was always hard, demanding, and painful. I had to learn a new mindset to get beyond the pain. That mindset was joy. Not happiness—I don't really remember that many practices that were happy occasions. But I do remember the joy of running with the whistle of the air blowing in my ears. I do remember the joy of making ten free throws at the end of practice so I could go home. I do remember the joy of making a defensive stop, then hitting the outlet pass that helped us score just a few seconds later.

Just like the process of learning to enjoy the hard work it took to play basketball, I needed to learn that the same was true in my everyday life. I needed to learn how to consider the hard parts of life as "pure joy" if I was to achieve the disciplines necessary to participate at an acceptable level.

We all have trials. To prove it I give you one word: puberty. That is a universal trial. Here, let me give a you a few more just to make my point:

- When people you love let you down
- When you're misunderstood
- When you don't have enough money
- When you have too much money (Oh, to have that trial!)
- Not liking something about your body ("I don't like my *fill-in-the-blank*")
- Mean people
- Thieves
- Friends who turn out to not be friends
- When things break
- When you feel insecure
- When you lose a loved one
- When you get your first child
- When you get your second . . . or third . . . child

We all have trials, and we will always have trials. But look back over that list and think about those items you identify most with. I think you will find that during those trials, you became stronger than at times when life was grand.

You will spend very few moments at the summit of the mountain you climb, and very few lessons will be learned there. It is in the climb out of the valley that the most personal growth is achieved. It is also where the greatest risks are taken. But if you linger too long at the top of the mountain, it'll be the greatest mistake you could ever make. You must keep climbing—for the pure joy of climbing.

TESTING: YOUR WORKBENCH TO ACHIEVE GREATNESS!

Many trials can be leveraged into the testing of your faith. This occurs when your trails take on a much greater meaning in your life. Our Creator has written our story, and it is a story just for us. In this storyline, the Creator has placed just the right obstacles to sharpen us for even greater victories. Testing of your faith is the pressure the Master Potter applies to the lump of clay to make a useful masterpiece by His design.

My first introduction to this concept as an adult occurred at a youth pastors' conference. I had shown up ready to quit the ministry. I hadn't been a youth pastor a long time—almost a full year. I told my story to a national youth leader who was leading the conference. I had a good story of "woe is me." My story usually got several "Oh, my"s and a couple "You're kidding"s. When I looked at this giant in the field of youth ministry, he was laughing at me.

When I confronted him, he just said, "I'm sorry, but if God has you going through this much this soon, you must be somebody special! God must have some great plans for you!" Then he pointed me to James Chapter 1:

> *Consider it pure joy, my brothers and sisters, whenever you face trials of many kinds, because you know that the testing of your faith produces perseverance. Let perseverance finish its work so that you may be mature and complete, not lacking anything.*

> James 1:2-4

I wanted to quit. But God wanted me to learn perseverance. I needed to change my perspective. Life wasn't happening *to* me; it was happening *for* me. God had written these events into my story before the foundation of the world. He was going to use my pain, if I worked through it, to move me closer to the designs He had for me. Closer to a more mature and complete version of me. The version of me who knew I was enough and that I had enough to make a difference.

The testing of our faith is meant to guide us into our blessings. When you see these difficult times as a gift, you can begin to experience joy.

> *Blessed is the one who perseveres under trial because, having stood the test, that person will receive the crown of life that the Lord has promised to those who love him.*
>
> James 1:12

James goes on to state the reward for persevering under trials and standing the tests that are sent our way. So many of us give up just before we see results. One of the rewards for not quitting while under a trial is the crown of life.

While I can't give you details about your crown of life, I do know that your crown is especially designed for you. You will receive this crown in heaven. However, I believe you can begin to receive portions of this reward here in this life. As you begin to conform to the design God has for you, you will receive the blessings of life. The life God intended for you can be yours as you conform to God's intended purpose, He has for you.

You need only to ask the Creator for wisdom to gain this new perspective of life. But you must ask in faith. Fear and doubt destroy this perspective and breed a perspective of negativity and death. James gives this advice to those who are having trouble with considering it pure joy when they face these situations.

If any of you lacks wisdom, you should ask God, who gives generously to all without finding fault, and it will be given to you. But when you ask, you must believe and not doubt, because the one who doubts is like a wave of the sea, blown and tossed by the wind. That person should not expect to receive anything from the Lord. Such a person is double-minded and unstable in all they do.

James 1:5-8

To find stability in your life you need to ask God and believe. We once again are revisiting the See and Believe Gates in this land of the Dare Gate. Do you dare to lean into the waves and winds? It is for the joy of life, the crown of life, that you lean into your pain to engage the design the Creator has made you for. Your story is mapped out to be a guide, an assistant, an encouragement to pursue God.

TEMPTATION: THE LURE TO ESCAPE OUR PAIN!

Temptation is when you look for an easy way out from the pain of your trials and testing. When you create avenues to short-circuit your pain, you will miss God's purpose for you. This divergent path has a very unpopular name: sin.

Sin is any detour from the story God has planned for your life. It means "to miss the mark." God has a perfect plan for your life. However, we all have strayed from that path. This has caused an emptiness within our souls. This emptiness is the source of our desire to find our Dreams and begin the Quests we were designed for. The old-time evangelists called this "being convicted by the Holy Spirit."

It's nobody fault but your own. You make choices, and many of those choices are designed to ease the pain in your life. The irony is that these choices to ease our pain only deepen it. We then seek methods to numb our pain. As Kary

Oberbrunner states in his book *The Deeper Path*, "Numbing your pain is numbing your potential." James puts it this way:

> but each person is tempted when they are dragged away by their own evil desire and enticed. Then, after desire has conceived, it gives birth to sin; and sin, when it is full-grown, gives birth to death.

James 1:14-15

We cannot place blame on God, our circumstances, or others when we attempt to numb our pain, escape our pain, or go our own way. That temptation comes from deep within us. It starts as just a thought; then it becomes a plot. Next that passing thought and plan give birth to action. All of this in turn gives birth to our death—the emptiness we feel dwelling in Ordinary.

James delivered a tough message to those who were in tough times. We all face tough times, and we also need this tough message: face trials with joy! Testing of your faith has great rewards. Need help with your perspective? Ask for wisdom to interpret your story correctly. Beware not to deceive yourself into thinking that you can escape pain. Escape will lead to separation from the Creator's path for you to find your Dream.

* * *

On my drive home from my short visit with Sandy in ICU, I asked God to help me understand the trials we both had been through in the last couple of years. It was not only the health issues, but the bills, and the loss of income, and the stress. It was hard to see where God was in all of this. It just didn't make sense. No more sense than taking my dad, mom, and brother from me.

I knew that I had received the message from the sky that read *Smile, God Loves You* and *Trust Jesus*. Sure, that was a neat story, but I needed something again. I needed to adjust my perspective—again.

It wasn't long before I began to hear within my heart the message of peace and hope. *I made you for this. You are designed for just such storms. In fact, I have written these storms with the wind and the waves to show you just how extraordinary your life is. Trust Me! I know what you can take, and I will gain glory from your story.* While it was not an audible voice, the message was clear. It was the message that God had been giving me for years now through His Word. The pain of my situation began to give way to the peace of my relationship with my Creator. I was receiving victory over the pain, even though it remained with me. I was reminded that I am on my Dream Quest. I had re-Awakened to my design.

* * *

THE DREAMER'S JOURNAL

Katie Champagne was born without hands on September 9, 1994. Her mother, Michelle Champagne, held her daughter in the hospital, feeling sad. She rubbed Katie's cheek, thinking, *How sad it is that she'll never be able to grab and touch me.* Michelle tells what happened next:

> *She then pinned my hand between her arms and touched my cheek. At that moment, I knew there was nothing this child wasn't going to be able to do with her life.*

Although Katie was born without hands, she has never seen herself as being disabled. In high school, she was the co-captain of the Oxford High School Equestrian Team. She rode her quarter horse in the state finals. That would be inspiring enough on its own, but she didn't stop there. She is able to perform any of the tasks anybody else performs each day. As a matter of fact, she can text message and use a smart phone faster than I can.

Oh, did I mention she is my niece's daughter? Because of the age difference between my brother and me, Katie's mom is more like a sister than a niece. I am very close to the Champagne family.

But there is much more to tell about Katie. She is a graduate of Michigan State University with a major in art. Her paintings have received critical acclaim, and she has artwork on permanent display at the MSU Library. She was also the art director for a software company while attending college full-time. She does inspirational speaking with her mother to youth and women's groups.

She is the embodiment of the statement, "Life doesn't happen to you, but for you."

One fall weekend, our families were together. A trip to the pumpkin patch set into motion a pumpkin carving contest among my five daughters and the three Champagne children. There were all sorts of sharp instruments being used among the teenage carvers. Excitement filled the room. It looked like Katie was one of the front-runners, but my daughters were determined to beat her. At the height of the carving, Katie made a slip with a knife, and it hit her in the eye. We all reacted with instant protection for her, and both her mom and dad were at her side in a flash. My youngest dropped her knife and reached to comfort and protect Katie. We all took a couple of steps in her direction to come to her aid. She covered her eye and ran to her room. Michelle and Doug (her dad) followed her.

What happened next was a total surprise to our family, but no surprise to the Champagnes. After making sure she was not injured, Katie came out of her bedroom, picked up the same knife, and went back to carving. She won the contest with that act of determination. Her confidence blew us away.

(By the way, she would have won even if she hadn't jabbed her eye with a knife. Her pumpkin was a true piece of art.)

Katie is married now. She is still close with her parents, Doug and Michelle. Jordan, Katie's husband, works with her in the software company and is finishing his education in Biblical Counseling.

All I can say is that she is one of my heroes.

PART 4

TO DO—ACTIVATING!

Tripp has gained great confidence in the Land beyond the Dare Gate. He has taken the clarity he gained in the Land of Dream and the competence he gained in the Land of Believe and coupled them together to build confidence and courage.

Alva has proven to be a great guide and companion in this land of unexpected roadblocks, setbacks, and detours. What Tripp can't get over is that, most of the time, his enemies are the falsehoods, fears, and self-limiting beliefs he has brought with him from Ordinary. He is learning to replace these with truth, courage, and a healthy awareness of his place in the world. This gives him great confidence to face the trials beyond the Dare Gate.

Tripp rides atop a black horse, reading the papers from within the pouch Alva gave him and planning his next adventure. It has been several years since he received the message in the pouch that the Creator had compiled for Tripp. Alva came across the pouch in a library, in the land beyond the Believe Gate. She recognized that this message was intended for Tripp, and delivered it to him before passing through the Dare Gate with him. The message contained the details of Tripp's design and story and outlined what his Dreamer's

141

Quest meant. It became a constant source of truth that Tripp meditated on as much as possible. Even during battle, Tripp learned the power of the words contained in these papers. Tripp realized that the words gave power to his Sword called Truth that was beyond his strength. They became his most important weapons.

He almost misses the Do Gate because he is busy making plans to begin his new life that is free of the obstacles of his old life in Ordinary. This gate is much more impressive than the other gates Tripp has encountered. There is a celestial look to this gate, with its spires and awesome proportions. The wall has a castle-like look, and Tripp sees there are dwellings within the wall occupied by what look like noblemen. The gate has a large sign with decorative doors that are secured in the open position. Tripp stops to ponder the gate. Tripp is intrigued by the very short message that sits atop the gate: *Do!*

If you look closely, the doors within the gate have two brass signs with ornate lettering. The first reads, *To Execute with Impact and Influence.* Then, under that sign, the other reads, *Love your Life, Live your Legacy—Today!*

As Tripp passes through the gate, he sees people immersed in the arts and trades of all sorts. The sight awakens his memories. This is the sight he caught brief glimpses of in the Land of the Dream Gate. This is the subject of study in the Land of the Believe gate, and it is the vision that was fought for in the Land of the Dare Gate. Tripp has a sense of arriving home as he investigates the various artisans at work here. Each one has a certain manner about them. It is hard for Tripp to determine if these specialists are at work or at play. Even the street vendors go about their tasks with an inner joy of fulfillment. Tripp quickly understands that the Land of Do is the place where travelers execute their vision, passion, and calling.

Tripp is now battle-tested and presents himself with a quiet confidence. Others take note of this traveler on a mission. He has quietly realized that he no longer longs to return to Ordinary. However, his Quest has brought him to a land adjacent to Ordinary. Tripp feels at home here and is considering making his home in the community named New Ordinary. It is a place where the elite travelers gather to recover from the stress they faced in the land beyond the Dare Gate. It is the place where Dreams are built, and imagination becomes reality. While exploring this new area, Tripp discovers that the Dreamer's Quest has brought him full circle. New Ordinary backs up to his old hometown of Ordinary.

While making this his new home, Trip has the sense that he is completing his Quest, yet also beginning it. He comes to realize that this is the land to activate his Dream. Like most, this realization comes in a flash when he finally comprehends that he now is able to execute his Dream.

As Tripp becomes more comfortable exploring the Land of Do, he notices a familiar gate close by. It is another Dream Gate. This gate has the same inscription written upon it: *To See with Clarity.* He does not hesitate to explore the lands beyond this gate. The journey is both enlightening and encouraging. He discovers some very familiar lands. However, the journey is easier and much quicker through these lands because he is equipped and prepared for what he will face.

There is a path through the Land of Dream leading to a new Believe Gate. It, too, has the same words as the other Believe Gate: *Observe with Competence.* It has the same Ivy League buildings that line its streets. This entrance opens onto the main street of the Land of Believe, and at the other end of that street is a third gate. It is a new Dare Gate. This one has the same words, *Master with Confidence,* etched into its doors. And of course, just to the horizon there is the fourth gate, the Do Gate, that brings Tripp back home to New Ordinary. This modern gate also has new words inscribed upon the doors, *Execute with Excellence!*

Tripp is still a traveler, a man on a Quest. With each new expedition he embarks upon by reentering the gates, he gains new insights about his Dreamer's Quest. This gives him even more confidence and courage to seek greater victories. And, with each journey, he expands his life more deeply than before. His legacy continues to grow.

Tripp is present in each day. He wastes no energy longing to relive the past or wishing for a better future. Tripp has united himself to the design of the Creator. He is whole, without the longing or the fear of missing out. Ever expanding his vision, he is content and comfortable with his present.

Tripp has had his Awakening! He has embarked on a boundless Dreamer's Quest that has become his model for life.

10

AWAKEN YOUR LEGACY

Just do what you do best.

Red Auerbach

* * *

It has happened to me many times: that moment when you see your Dream come to life before your eyes. You realize exactly why you are in this situation at this moment—to serve this person or group. It is the awareness that you are doing what you are designed to do.

There is a love that overtakes you in these moments. A love for those you serve. A love for your Creator for designing you for this moment. There is love for your life that also overtakes you. Words can only attempt to describe the depth of the feelings you experience at times like this.

I encounter way too many people who have never experienced this in their lives. I have also spoken to people who once had this contentment but lost it. Then there are the people who know exactly what I am talking about. Their moment of Awakening has been burned into their consciousness. They are able to repeat moments like this again and again.

I experienced a moment like this one evening as I looked out over our backyard filled with teens and adults. I was throwing a cookout and pool party for the student leaders and leadership teams in Lancaster, Pennsylvania, where I was a youth pastor. I had run into our house to retrieve something. When I turned and looked out the window, I was struck by the sight of teens and adults all enjoying each other's company. It was a picture of real community that only comes after you have served side by side.

I don't remember exactly what triggered me to pause and reflect upon the group at that moment. I do remember that they had a love, joy, and respect for each other, regardless of age or background, that still inspires me to this day. As I recalled our journey together—what we had accomplished, and were going to accomplish—I was humbled and overtaken with joy. I realized in that moment that God had given me my Dream. I was loving my life and living my legacy in that very moment.

Another one of these moments happened in New York City on a street evangelism trip. I was sitting on a park bench. My vision panned across the public park to see students and adults from my church, spread across the area. They were engaged in conversations with people from different walks, cultures, religions, and races. Some played chess with the local hustlers. Some played with children and spoke to their parents. Some offered food from their backpacks to people who lived on the streets. Some spoke with young people who were not much different from themselves, despite very different living conditions. And some spoke with people who they had little in common with, seeking to understand and to help if they could. In that flash, I knew I was made for this type of leadership. Again, I was loving my life and living my legacy.

There were the food collection efforts we organized each year around Thanksgiving, in whatever city we were living in. It was such a blessing to my soul to watch hundreds of volunteers bring food in and create care packages to make a Thanksgiving dinner.

Watching families receive their care packages was always fun. But my favorite was when parents would bring their children to help distribute the care packages around the community. To witness one generation passing on the importance of serving to the next generation always gave me a moment of joy. I was doing something right and real. Over the years, there have been thousands of care packages distributed as a result of Sandy's and my efforts. But I know with certainty that I received much more in return than I gave.

These moments happen when I stand in front of a group telling my stories, or when I deliver an important life-transforming message to a group or individual. Or the one-on-one conversations where I can help someone find hope in the lowest moments of their life. Or when I disclose my story to a couple who are facing struggles of their own. These are moments when my design and story merge together in meaning.

* * *

In Chapter 2, we left Joseph in prison. He was faithful to pursue his Dream where God had planted him. He was not a victim pointing blame at his family. He did not make excuses that he was not able to put his God-given talents to use. He never denied his Dream, declaring it unreasonable for him to achieve.

Rather than becoming a victim, he amassed victory after victory. He succeeded by taking ownership of his situation, applying his leadership skills to serve his master (in slavery) and his prison keeper (in captivity). He held himself to the highest standards of integrity. He took responsibility for his actions, never allowing himself to become detoured by the wrongs of others. Even in the face of betrayal, Joseph carved his own path, which would eventually lead him to his Dream.

Because of the lust and lies of his master's wife, Joseph was imprisoned. There he served the prison warden with honor. Soon he was elevated to being in the charge of the prison while remaining a prisoner.

In Genesis Chapter 40, some high-profile prisoners were put into his care. They were the royal cupbearer and the royal baker. We are not told what had landed these two high-ranking servants in prison. We are only told that they were placed in Joseph's custody. They were blessed to be placed in his care, because the love he bestowed upon the prisoners in his care was extraordinary.

One night, both men had disturbing dreams that left them bewildered the next morning. Joseph noticed that the men were dejected. He went to them and asked them why their faces were so sad. (Can you imagine an assistant warden asking a prisoner why they are sad-looking?) Joseph was a servant to everyone he had contact with. This servant heart had won him high standing in both slavery and imprisonment. He had gained influence because he served with compassion.

Pharaoh's servants told him that they'd both had dreams, but they did not understand the meaning. Joseph used this moment of distress to point the men to eternal answers. Joseph pointed out that God knows all things. He told the two men that he would ask God for the meaning of the dreams.

Eager to learn the interpretation of the dream, the cupbearer went first. He told a story of a grape vine that had three branches. On each of the branches were grapes. He squeezed the grapes into Pharaoh's cup and handed it to Pharaoh.

Joseph gave the interpretation: the three branches meant three days. He would be restored back into the service of Pharaoh, back into his old position. Joseph only asked that the cupbearer speak to Pharaoh about his situation in prison. The cupbearer agreed.

The baker, after hearing the positive interpretation of the cupbearer's dream, asked for Joseph to tell him what his dream meant. He was carrying three baskets of bread on his head to deliver to Pharaoh. But birds kept stealing the bread. Joseph quickly gave him the meaning of the dream. Three baskets meant three days. On the third day, Pharaoh would behead the baker and hang him from a tree. The birds would eat his body. Yikes! My guess is that the baker did not cheer up much after that discussion.

In three days, the meanings Joseph had given to each man occurred just as he said they would. However, the cupbearer quickly forgot about Joseph and his promise.

In Chapter 41 of Genesis we are told that, two years later, Pharaoh had two dreams. None of his court could understand the meaning of these dreams, which caused great stress in the palace. It was at this moment that the cupbearer remembered his time in prison. Maybe it would be worth the risk to tell Pharaoh now about Joseph.

Pharaoh summoned Joseph to be taken from the prison, cleaned up, and presented before him immediately. Pharaoh asked Joseph if he could tell the meaning of dreams. Again, Joseph was faithful to tell Pharaoh that no, he could not. Only God could give him the meaning. Pharaoh told Joseph his dreams.

In the first dream, there came seven cows up out of the Nile River. They were beautiful and fat. Then came seven ugly, skinny cows. They ate the first seven cows. In Pharaoh's second dream, there were seven beautiful stalks of grain. Then there appeared seven thin and scorched heads of grain. The thin heads of grain devoured the healthy, fat heads of grain.

Joseph spent a night in prayer about the dreams, asking God for help. He appeared before Pharaoh the next morning. They were both the same dream. God was telling Pharaoh that Egypt would have seven years of amazing harvests. But right after that, the country would enter a seven-year famine.

Pharaoh asked Joseph what recommendations he had for the peek into the future God had given him. Joseph advised Pharaoh to tax the plentiful seven-year harvest at 20 percent and to store the grain up for the uncertain future. Then in the seven years of famine, Pharaoh would have enough to feed Egypt. Pharaoh liked the plan, and Joseph found favor in his eyes. He placed Joseph second only to himself, to rule over Egypt during the years of prosperity and of the coming famine. Joseph was given Pharaoh's ring, a symbol that he had the power of Pharaoh himself to rule all Egypt.

Joseph must have had moments during the first seven years when it occurred to him that God had not abandoned him in the dried up well, or in slavery, or even in imprisonment. Genesis 41:50-52 tells us the blessing that came Joseph's way. First, Pharaoh gave Joseph a wife, Asenath, the daughter of Potiphera, a priest of On. We get a little insight into Joseph's mindset during the time of plenty in Egypt. Joseph was blessed with two sons, Manasseh and Ephraim. His selection of names for his sons tells the story.

"Manasseh" sounds like the Hebrew word "to forget." When naming his firstborn son, Joseph said, "It is because God has made me forget all my trouble and all my father's household." God had replaced anger and hurt with forgiveness of all who had wronged Joseph, including his family.

"Ephraim" sounds like the Hebrew word that means "twice fruitful." At the birth of his second son, Joseph said, "It is because God has made me fruitful in the land of my suffering." Joseph had pieced together that life doesn't happen to us, it happens for us.

Joseph must have often thought about the dream of his youth. Could he become a powerful ruler one day? And what was the meaning of his family members bowing to him? It was not until the famine, when Joseph's father and brothers were without the resources necessary to feed their family and flocks, that he would see the family connection.

The famine had affected the entire region. Jacob had heard that Egypt had food stores, so he sent his ten sons there to buy food. Because Jacob had lost his favorite son, Joseph, to wild animals (or so he believed), he was keeping his youngest son, Benjamin, close by his side. There would be no trip for Benjamin. So, the ten older sons of Jacob left for Egypt. Little did any of them know, they would be bowing to Joseph to gain their salvation from the famine. Genesis 42 through 50 tells a tale of restoration of a family beyond any story you will find in any movie—even a Hallmark movie!

Joseph was able to save his entire family from starvation by moving them to Egypt. He also restored his relationship with his brothers, who had sold him into slavery and told their father that Joseph had been killed by a wild animal.

It took several trips to Egypt before Joseph revealed his identity to his brothers. His brothers could not fathom the fact that Joseph forgave them—that he wanted to serve them rather than destroy them. His ten older brothers had used their power over Joseph to conspire to destroy him.

Joseph had learned that power and influence are tools to serve others. When somebody uses them as tools to only build their empire, they tend to lose the influence they once had. It becomes an ugly mess that that must be covered up, like Joseph's brothers had done for years.

Then Jacob died. The ten brothers became gripped with distress yet again about their malicious behavior toward their brother. They feared that Joseph had been restrained by Jacob from seeking revenge. They could only imagine the horrible plot Joseph had in mind for them. Even though he had brought them to Egypt and given them a life of abundance, they still could not grasp the mindset of forgetting and being twice fruitful (the meanings of the names of Joseph's two sons) when you receive your Dream.

Still fearing Joseph's wrath, his brothers devised one more plan to save their necks. They sent word that Jacob, before his death, had left a message with them to give to Joseph.

When Joseph's brothers saw that their father was dead, they said, "What if Joseph holds a grudge against us and pays us back for all the wrongs we did to him?" So they sent word to Joseph, saying, "Your father left these instructions before he died: 'This is what you are to say to Joseph: I ask you to forgive your brothers the sins and the wrongs they committed in treating you so badly.' Now please forgive the sins of the servants of the God of your father." When their message came to him, Joseph wept.

His brothers then came and threw themselves down before him. "We are your slaves," they said.

Genesis 50:15-18

This happened after they had carried out the burial instructions Jacob had left them. Joseph had traveled to Canaan with the entire family to bury the body there. Then they traveled back to Egypt to live their lives without Jacob. The message that Joseph receives reveals the fear in his brothers. Joseph weeps for his family.

But Joseph said to them, "Don't be afraid. Am I in the place of God? You intended to harm me, but God intended it for good to accomplish what is now being done, the saving of many lives. So then, don't be afraid. I will provide for you and your children." And he reassured them and spoke kindly to them.

Genesis 50:19-21

It is important to note Joseph's answer. There you will find the Dreamer's Quest explained. Even when others mean to harm you, God means for those events to be for good in your life. He has already written your story in His book. When pursuing your Dream, the purpose of your life, it is important that you give room for even the bad events in your life to be used by God for good ends.

Finally, even with the ongoing wounds of mistrust that Joseph endured from his brothers, he continued to serve them. He reassured them. He spoke kindly to them. Joseph had come to understand his original Dream about his brothers bowing to him was misinterpreted to mean they would be his servants. The opposite was true, Joseph was to be their servant. Leadership is about serving. It is not about receiving, but about giving.

When you think about rags-to-riches stories, this one has to make your Top Ten List. The dream that Joseph had as a child had now fallen into place. It was not a Dream to become a master, but to become a servant. It was not about conquest, but about saving lives. It was not about taking the place of God but taking the place of serving God.

* * *

During my youth, I thought leadership was about being the boss. I have come to realize it is about making a difference in people's lives. And influence and impact come as a result of understanding the needs of others and meeting them. It's more about listening than telling. It's more about understanding than bossing. It's more about positive input than negative feedback.

As a boy and into my adult life, I had such a distorted image of leaders that I would lash out at authority. I rejected the thought that the Creator might have given me leadership skills. And it never occurred to me that leadership would be part of my Dream.

But it was in moments of servant leadership that I found the greatest fulfillment in my life. I found that when I used my gifts to help others in need, I felt a deep love for my life and a joy in fulfilling my legacy. I wanted to repeat those moments again and again.

The fulfillment of the Dreamer's Quest is found in:

- Discovery of your design to achieve your Dream

    o Dream: To See with Clarity

- Understanding the rules to execute your story effectively to reach your Dream

    o Believe: To Observe with Competence

- Conquering the obstacles that impede your progress toward your Dream

    o Dare: To Master with Confidence

- Achieving a lifestyle that lets you pursue your Dream and equips you to serve others

    o Do: To Execute with Influence and Impact

Awakening! The Dreamer's Quest is about the journey you must take to discover, understand, conquer, and achieve the important things in life. You are designed for greatness within your Dream. Your Dream is very specific to you. Only you can accomplish your Dream. Only you can make a difference in many lives by living your Dream today!

As I move forward in my Dreamer's Quest, I find myself aligning to my original design and purpose, given to me by the Creator. I *see with clarity* my story as written by God. God is enabling me to forgive, to forget, and to receive His blessings.

I pursue knowledge and skills *to observe with competence* the areas that need development to better align with my purpose or Dream.

I *master with confidence* the skills I have learned so I can confront the roadblocks and setbacks I encounter on my Quest.

I *execute with influence and impact.* I enjoy a life I love, and I live my legacy every day. As I experience this joy of life, I want more of it. I revisit each of the four gates to discover, understand, conquer, and achieve even more within my Dream.

* * *

THE DREAMER'S JOURNAL

I already introduced you to my father, Charles Hershel Johnson. He left no great inheritance to his family. If we could measure society's standard of greatness with a radar, he would only be a small blip on the screen. Like I said, he had little wealth, little power, and little popularity. There are no social media pages that would say he even existed. No Wikipedia entries about him.

Yet, I believe him to be the perfect example of loving your life. And, towards the end of his life, he lived each day pursuing his Dream.

He served his wife. Even in the face of great obstacles and setbacks, he loved her like he loved himself. He cared for her. He provided for her. He gave her the best whenever possible. He also served his family. He was quick to come visit or to move close to one of his sons. He would always find a project to complete for them.

He loved to study the Bible. Not just read it, but to dig deep into theology to discover the truth about God and his plan for us. It was not unusual for me to receive a phone call from dad during the day, while I was at my church office. He would have some deep question about theology that would give a seminary student a headache. I would have to dig out one of the theology books I had access to to try and answer his question.

He would often say to me, "Godliness with contentment is great gain." He was by no means a perfect man. We had our disagreements. These would hurt him deeply. However, he had a hard time finding the words to make things right. Many times, he would even make things worse. I think it was because of the lack of parental input into his life. While he loved us deeply, he always found it hard to express that love.

But he had found the secret. He loved his life and he lived his legacy each day while he was still with us. As I pointed out before, he was an ordinary man. But he was also an extraordinary man. He had found what God had designed him to do. To care for his family by living an example of how we are to live—to grow, overcome, and discover. Directing all things to God for his glory.

11

ACCOMPLISH YOUR CALLING

Earn your success based on service to others, not at the expense of others.

H. Jackson Brown Jr.

* * *

Every action you take, every word you speak, is another building block of the brand called "you."

Did you make forts in your childhood? I did. I would dream of making a stockade deep within the wilderness, with a log cabin that had a view of the mountains. Or maybe it was a grass-roofed hut on my own island, with an endless supply of food from the ocean that surrounded me. What can I say? I always dreamed big! It didn't matter if I didn't have the resources—I knew I could always dream.

Many times, after I had a dream in mind, I would look around for materials to bring my vision into reality. As a boy, I enjoyed building forts, which became 3-D expressions of my dreams. I would sometimes make sketches of my forts. Other times, I would become inspired by a board or a stick or a pile of snow and go to work.

When my mom was away, I would sometimes take all the sheets and blankets I could find and build a tent fort in the living room. This activity did not please my mom. If my dad was the first to arrive home, he would tell me to get things back in order before my mom saw what I had done. Then he would go about his usual routine, leaving me to the honor system. That meant I had a little more time to live in my dream. This would last until my mom returned to put a stop to the "foolishness." She usually made me take everything to the laundry to be cleaned for the guests we never seemed to have.

I was always on the lookout for more durable building materials. If I could get my hands of a refrigerator box, that was gold! Not only could I build a structure from it, I could draw on the outside and inside. I could make it look like what I imagined it to be: anything from a frontier fort to a spaceship. But cardboard did not stand up to the adventures of a young boy for very long.

As time went on, I graduated from childhood to adult forts. There were the hunting blinds that my brothers and I built in the forest to hunt deer. These structures moved from simple forts of branches and logs to tree stands made from wood pallets with two-by-four ladders nailed to the side of the tree. Next, we purchased manufactured tree stands that we mounted high within trees overlooking deer trails. Finally, we graduated to building structures with shingle roofs, glass windows that slid silently open, locking doors, and garages to park the four-wheeler under the elevated one-room man fort. We even had stairs, carpet, and heat inside.

Next, I expanded into building a funhouse each year for the youth group in Fremont. Each fall, the guys on the youth staff would spend evenings and weekends in September and October transforming a barn into what slightly resembled the Haunted Mansion at Disney. We ran hundreds of students through this labor of love at the annual fall party.

I finally moved to building the ultimate fort—a house for my family. Sandy and I had four children at the time. We were renting half of a small house, with two bedrooms and one bathroom, located behind the local Dairy Queen. We were so close to the Dairy Queen that the drive-through was almost at our back door. On several occasions, when I called our dog to come in with, "Here, Lady! Here, Lady!" I would hear the drive-through speaker answer, "Welcome to Dairy Queen, may I take your order." This became great fun—but the house was much too small and not fun at all.

I searched for housing solutions for several months, only to come up empty. I spent an hour or two every day looking into rentals or searching for some way to buy a house with no money down. I was determined to make our Dream of owning a house a reality.

I came home one day and said, "I'm going to build a house!" Now, understand: my wife, Sandy, is my biggest fan. But that day must have been unusually hard, being coped up with four children in that tiny house. She came back quickly with, "Yeah, right!"

With no money in hand but with lots of prayer, I approached a businessman from our church to see if I could secure a building lot from him. Not knowing if he even had property to sell, I made my pitch. He told me he was looking into developing part of his farm. He offered two different locations for us to consider. The next day we purchased two acres of land for $1.00. That's right, that's not a typo, $1.00.

I used the free-and-clear deed to the lot as down payment to build a 2,400 square foot house and a three-car garage. A little over a year later, we had completed the task. (Notice I said that *I* was going to build the house, but *we* completed it.) As I moved forward in building this dream house, I learned that the right plans, materials, and tools combined with the right team make an enduring structure.

What really made this work was that I created a brand for myself—builder. The first person I sold my brand to was Sandy, my wife. She saw my many tree stands and my funhouses go from ideas to reality. While she needed some convincing, she bought into my new brand of "builder."

Then I sold that same brand to the landowner, the banker, the subcontractors, and the volunteer workers I assembled to build the house. The idea that a pastor could build a house on his own took some effort to sell.

Everybody has a brand. It is the identity that you believe about yourself, that you communicate through your attitudes. People are examining your brand to see if it is consistent with your actions. If it is, you can assemble a team to make your Dream a reality.

When you set out to build your Dream, you may need to create a new brand for yourself. People are watching you, and they already have an image of what your brand is—what you are known for. You will need to consider several questions about yourself:

- Is it obvious to others exactly what your Dream is?

- When people think about you, do they see the connection between you and your Dream?

- How does your Dream serve others? If it does not serve others, then you may have confused a Dream for a desire. (I may want to retire one day, which is fine, and a worthy goal, but that is not a Dream. To retire so I can become more engaged in serving my grandchildren is a Dream. There is an object to the desire besides yourself.)

* * *

PART 4: TO DO—ACTIVATING!

In ancient times, corporations had not come into existence. Society was organized into kingdoms, tribes, and families. Take, for example, Israel. Jacob, who God named Israel (Gen. 32:28, 35:10) fathered twelve sons, who became fathers to twelve families, which became the twelve tribes of Israel. These twelve tribes became the foundation for the nation of Israel, the nation promised to Abraham and Isaac (Jacob's grandfather and father). Their story became a story respected throughout the entire known world. If I may use a modern word, their reputation became their brand.

Ruth, a Moabite woman, became a very important figure in the national story of Israel. Her commitment to her husband's family was put to the test. Would she continue to take the name of her family by marriage, or would she retreat to her family of heritage? The importance of this decision would not only be an example of a family's love, but it would become a keystone to the national story of Israel. Hers is a story of how famine and death—seemingly bad events—are part of our redemption story.

In an unusual twist for a story from antiquity, this story begins with a woman. Women during this time usually did not own land, nor did they usually earn enough to meet their needs without a father or a husband to care for them. Naomi, and her two daughters-in-law, Orpah and Ruth, had lost their husbands in a matter a few years. Naomi had lost her husband Elimelech while they lived in Moab. Elimelech had moved his wife and two sons there from Bethlehem to escape a famine. While living there, his two sons took wives from Moab.

Some time later, Elimelech died, leaving Naomi with her two sons and their wives. After ten years, both sons passed away, leaving Naomi, Orpah, and Ruth widows. After hearing that the famine had ended in Bethlehem, and Naomi decided to move back home.

Orpah and Ruth both decided to stay with Naomi and move to Bethlehem also. However, Naomi released them to go back to their homes, to remarry and have families of their own. Orpah chose to return to her mother's house. There was a time of weeping together for their loss and for saying their goodbyes. Meanwhile, Ruth made to commitment to stay with Naomi and to travel to Bethlehem, the home of her passed husband and her mother-in-law.

While Orpah decided to take back the branding of her birth parents, "Moabite," Ruth decided to take on the branding of Elimelech, "Ephrathite" (a group within the tribe of Judah, within the nation of Israel). Naomi urged her one more time to reconsider and return to her family in Moab. Ruth made clear her commitment to remain part of Naomi's family:

> *But Ruth replied, "Don't urge me to leave you or to turn back from you. Where you go, I will go, and where you stay, I will stay. Your people will be my people and your God my God. Where you die, I will die, and there I will be buried. May the* LORD *deal with me, be it ever so severely, if even death separates you and me." When Naomi realized that Ruth was determined to go with her, she stopped urging her.*

Ruth 1:16-18

The two women went to Bethlehem to face life as widows together. Ruth quickly went to work, providing for the needs of the two women by gleaning (gathering grain or the like) behind the harvesters in the fields, a privilege reserved for widows in Israel. Naomi pointed her in the right direction, and she found favor in the eyes of Boaz, a younger brother of Elimelech and an uncle of Ruth's dead husband.

Boaz had heard Ruth's story and took notice of her hard work to support herself and Naomi. He invited her to eat lunch with his workers, giving her enough food to fill herself and to take home food to Naomi. He suggested she continue to glean his fields behind his harvesters. He also instructed his harvesters to leave extra grain on the ground for her to pick up.

She returned home with almost a bushel of grain and the food provided for her during lunch. She also described to Naomi how Boaz had aided them. Naomi instructed her to stick with the plan of following Boaz's harvesters. She also took note that Boaz had heard her story and that he was assisting Ruth's efforts to support herself and Naomi.

There was another, older brother of Elimelech who had a controlling interest, by birthright, in Elimelech's property. During this time in history, women very rarely controlled real estate on their own. However, Naomi put into action a plan to secure both her and Ruth's future. Ruth would approach Boaz to become the "kinsman-redeemer" for Elimelech.

To fulfill the kinsman-redeemer role, one would purchase the dead man's estate and take his widow in marriage so an heir could be born in the deceased husband's name. If there were more than one living brother, the oldest was first in line to fulfill the kinsman-redeemer role. If he decided not to fulfill the role, he could pass it to another brother. In this case, Naomi had two sons who carried the family name forward. After both brothers died and only one daughter-in-law remained to carry on the family legacy, it fell to Ruth to continue the family name.

Some time later, Ruth was instructed by Naomi to find where Boaz was camped during harvest, and to wait until he had finished his work for the day, had dinner, and fallen asleep. Then, Ruth was to go sleep at his feet. If he covered her with the corner of his blanket, it would be a sign that he accepted the role of kinsman-redeemer.

Ruth did as she was instructed. Boaz was startled awake during the night and discovered Ruth sleeping at his feet. He offered her a corner of his covers to show his intensions. Before day break, he told her to return to Naomi.

The next morning, Boaz approached his brother in front of the town elders. He suggested that his brother buy Elimelech's property. His brother said he would do it that day. Then Boaz told him that to buy the property he had to marry Ruth as the kinsman-redeemer. Becoming the kinsman-redeemer would put his other properties in jeopardy, so the brother gave the rights to Boaz, who immediately took on the responsibility.

What does this story have to do with brand?

First, Ruth still carried the brand of "Moabite," but she was the wife of an Israelite. After the deaths of both Elimelech and Mahlon, she had a choice: to take back her identity as a Moabite, or to move with Naomi back to Bethlehem, taking on the identity of an Israelite daughter to her. Her marriage to Mahlon was her Dream, and she was going to stick with it.

Second, she had to learn a new culture. She became immersed in the Jewish culture. She acted on the Jewish laws by observing these laws. She gained competence in the life of her Dream, and others saw evidence of her commitment.

Third, her proclamation was not only backed by her actions, but her confidence in her decision became evident to outside observers. Her competence led to confident action, which was blessed with a better option.

Fourth, this led to a beautiful love story with a man of means who could ensure the fulfillment of her Dream. When Boaz became Ruth's kinsman-redeemer, she secured her place in the national history of Israel. Her brand is forever sealed in the legacy of her new family.

Not only is Ruth the great-grandmother of David, the giant-killing warrior king of Israel, and man after God's own heart, but she is also listed in the linage of Jesus (Matthew 1:5). Both the Jewish and Christian faiths have important ties to the decision that Ruth made. She saw with clarity (to go where Naomi went), observed with competence (to do as Naomi instructed her), and mastered with confidence (to bring home food to Naomi), and she stepped into her Dream (to marry Boaz and continue the family line). It was along this path that her Dream became her brand.

* * *

I have always been a dreamer. As a boy, I would create imaginary worlds. I would be the fireman who ran into the burning forest, the sports hero who made the important play for a team victory, or the air traffic controller who guided hundreds of planes to safety. I was a builder, explorer, and discoverer of innovative concepts. My imagination was always working.

I learned that I was built to handle difficult circumstances that others would avoid. I was good in situations that pressured me to take decisive action. I loved building teams to reach goals. I thrived on projects that required creative thinking, innovation, and discovery of methods to build new systems from imagination to completion.

It was when I doubted my callings that I developed issues of poor self-esteem, lack of confidence, and the loss of ability to make decisions and act. During these times I felt helpless. I wandered through my problems not seeing the opportunity they laid before me.

It would take an Awakening to jolt me back into remembering who I was. I was designed by the Creator to win. My story was written before I ever drew my first breath. It is a story in which I find hope, peace, joy and meaning. It is a Quest to take hold of my legacy. When I did, I loved my life and lived the legacy I was designed for.

Our Dreams, expressed by our lives, become our brand. Like Ruth, we are all designed for a specific purpose in life. A purpose that only we can fulfill. And when we step into that role, we find the fulfillment we had longed for our whole lives.

As I contemplate my Quest, it has been a journey filled with twists and turns. From the family I was born into, to the privileges of being part of my family, to the hardships that I endured, to the deep friendships I made, to the experiences I had and the decisions I made—it all adds up to a meaningful life. Not always the easiest life, but each piece adds significance to a life driven by a Dream within. The Creator has been alongside me every step of the way—guiding and empowering me into greater meaning. That meaning is found in service to God and others. (Matthew 22: 36-40)

The Dreamer's Quest goes much deeper than pursuing our wants or desires. The subject of the Dream is others, not yourself. When we live our Dream, we will help others as we find fulfillment. To merely seek a lifestyle of self-service will never satisfy the deep longing within your soul.

Judas was the follower of Jesus who was entrusted with the funds of Jesus' ministry. He became consumed with a desire to serve himself. John, the beloved disciple, tells this story about Judas:

Then Mary took about a pint of pure nard, an expensive perfume; she poured it on Jesus' feet and wiped his feet with her hair. And the house was filled with the fragrance of the perfume.

But one of his disciples, Judas Iscariot, who was later to betray him, objected, "Why wasn't this perfume sold and the money given to the poor? It was worth a year's wages." He did not say this because he cared about the poor but because he was a thief; as keeper of the money bag, he used to help himself to what was put into it.

John 12:3-6

I'm sure that, at some point in time, Judas had a passion to meet the needs of the poor. Otherwise the group wouldn't have placed the money bag in his control. But his passion moved from serving others to serving himself. This paved the way for his ultimate betrayal of Jesus for thirty pieces of silver. However, trying to find fulfillment in silver led to him taking his own life.

We must take great care to use our passion to serve others rather than ourselves. It can make the difference between a life ending in fulfillment or a life ending in disappointment.

Ruth made the decision to remain with Naomi. She made the choice to commit to a Dream deep within her soul, to be part of the nation of Israel. She made a pledge to follow Naomi, to make Naomi's God her God. Then she was careful to learn the new lifestyle of her new identity. She stood up to the setbacks that stood in her path. She lived her Dream—her legacy—and she loved her life.

* * *

THE DREAMER'S JOURNAL

The injustice of racism, held over from before the founding of the United States, was accepted as a norm. The ugly behaviors were deeply embedded into our social fabric by years of slave trading. Fortunes were built upon the backs of those who had little or nothing to offer. Rather than to use their wealth to serve humanity, the rich would enslave the helpless to amass even more riches for themselves. Even among some Christian groups, these beliefs had become acceptable. We needed a leader with clarity to see the injustice and to guide us to a new era of hope for all people.

Martin Luther King Jr. was an American Baptist minister who changed the fabric of America's thinking. He began his public movement in 1955 by leading the Montgomery bus boycott. This opened the opportunity for him to start and lead the Southern Christian Leadership Conference. These events would lead to the March on Washington in 1963, where he delivered his famous "I Have A Dream" speech. Many would say this speech changed the course of the Civil Rights movement—and, ultimately, the values in the USA and around the world. Here is that speech:

I say to you today, my friends, so even though we face the difficulties of today and tomorrow, I still have a dream. It is a dream deeply rooted in the American dream.

I have a dream that one day this nation will rise up and live out the true meaning of its creed: 'We hold these truths to be self-evident: that all men are created equal.'

I have a dream that one day on the red hills of Georgia the sons of former slaves and the sons of former slave owners will be able to sit down together at the table of brotherhood.

I have a dream that one day even the state of Mississippi, a state sweltering with the heat of injustice, sweltering with the heat of oppression, will be transformed into an oasis of freedom and justice.

I have a dream that my four little children will one day live in a nation where they will not be judged by the color of their skin but by the content of their character.

I have a dream today.

I have a dream that one day, down in Alabama, with its vicious racists, with its governor having his lips dripping with the words of interposition and nullification; one day right there in Alabama, little black boys and black girls will be able to join hands with little white boys and white girls as sisters and brothers. I have a dream today.[3]

Martin Luther King Jr. led the fight against segregation, racism and Jim Crow laws that keep a race of people from pursuing their Dreams. He used nonresistance, peaceful marches, and protests to revive the nation's beliefs. He was always in the service of his Dream, never self-promoting. In 1968 he was assassinated in Memphis, Tennessee. However, his Dream is alive today. Martin Luther King Jr.'s Dream continues to light the truth that "all men are created equal."

---

[3] King, Martin L., Jr. "I Have a Dream." Speech. Lincoln Memorial, Washington, D. C. 28 Aug. 1963. *American Rhetoric*, 25 Mar. 2013, https://www.americanrhetoric.com/speeches/mlkihaveadream.htm

12

ASSEMBLE YOUR TEAM

Take heed, then, often to come together to give thanks to God, and show forth His praise. For when you assemble frequently in the same place, the powers of Satan are destroyed, and the destruction at which he aims is prevented by the unity of your faith.

Ignatius of Antioch

* * *

Over a lifetime of Awakening, my Dreamer's Quest has been aided by so many people that I could never list them all here. If I tried, I would fail, because God has used so many to help shape me and my Dream. He used teachers who saw something within me that nobody else saw and placed me into situations to discover and grow. He used leaders who caught a glimpse of some trait that needed to be developed within me. He used family members who lovingly suffered through my bad decisions. Then there are the many preachers, teachers, speakers, and thought leaders who have spoken or written their messages.

Then there are the "negative" people who I owe a debt of gratitude. They taught me in the school of hard knocks. They gave me even greater resolve to pursue my Dream. They allowed me to rise to the occasion and overcome the injustices that they brought into my life. One life lesson I have learned from books, movies, and graphic novels is this: to have a great hero, you must have a great villain. Many times, the villain helps shape the hero. While "villain" may seem a harsh term, I am thankful for those who opposed my Dream along the way. They gave me great strength to keep moving forward.

I spent too much time being defensive about my Dreamer's Quest. There were times when I allowed anger, depression, or insecurity to overtake my passion for my Dream. I would blame others for my own opportunities for growth. I would make excuses for my shortcomings as a person. Or, worst of all, I would deny that I had any culpability in my lack of progress toward my purpose in life.

These self-inflicted wounds would manifest in anger. It was ugly behavior that only moved me farther away from my goals. Or I would become depressed, thinking that I was not worthy to achieve my Dream. There were times when I lacked confidence and became too paralyzed to make any forward progress in my Dreamer's Quest.

This started early in life. Some of my most public examples occurred on the basketball court in high school and college, and then in adult leagues. I was so insecure that, if a coach corrected me, I would lose it. Even worse, if a ref made a call against me, I would see it as a put-down of my abilities and stomp around the court. Any mention of wrongdoing could spark a moment of rage. This carried into my adult life, not only with basketball, but any other activity that I loved to do.

Outbursts of anger also occurred in the classroom. Any hint of red marks on tests or papers would send me into a rage. I had to be as close to perfect as I possibly could be. The very thought of attempting a project could send me into a deep depression. I would take these feelings of depression and turn them into excuses for not beginning or completing the Dreamer's Quest the Creator had placed within me.

Close behind the depression would be the insecurity. Always at the ready, it would give me an excuse to withdraw. I let my false interpretations of myself override my Creator's design and the story he had entrusted me with.

My anger and withdrawal would drive away the people who wanted to see me succeed in my Quest. My coaches, teachers—and, yes, even the refs who made the calls against me—all really wanted to see me achieve my goals. Teammates would withdraw from me because I did not show a willingness to listen. This made me even more insecure, which led to a downward spiral of more anger, which led to more rejection.

But I had some stubborn family, friends, and mentors who would let nothing sway them from their love for me. They stuck with me. They saw something within me that I couldn't. They would not allow me to stay stuck for very long. Our confrontations were sometimes heated, but they would convince me that I was going the wrong direction.

It was through this process that I began to love my "team." By that, I mean the group of people I knew would keep me grounded. Even if I didn't deserve it or want it, they would make sure I heard the truth. I cannot describe to you how much I owe these people. I have such respect for them. It's beyond my comprehension how they put up with my foolish behavior. "Grateful" is just the beginning of the feelings I have for them.

I want to be a part of as many people's teams as possible. In fact, this calling has become the opening phrase to my life mission statement, *To influence and impact as many people as possible* . . . While traveling the roads of the Dreamer's Quest, I have become a collector of people. I want to give the love, acceptance, and guidance God placed in my life to as many people as possible. I want to give them what others gave to me:

the skills to Dream; to Believe; to Dare; to Do; to Be. These have become the key components to my Dreamer's Quest.

Some use the word "tribe." Others, "their family." I like "team." I want not only to build into the lives of the people I encounter, but also to allow them to build into my life as well. I know that my Dream is not the same as other people's. If I help them pursue their Dreams—to experience Awakening— chances are, they will be an expert in some area I need help with. The larger the team, the more ability you will have to meet the needs each of you has on your Dreamer's Quest.

* * *

It was around 445 BC, and Artaxerxes was king of Persia. He ruled much of what we know as the Middle East. In his employ was a very high-ranking official who was an Israelite. Nehemiah was the cupbearer to the king. This would be akin to being the head of the Secret Service that guards the President of the United States. He was one of the king's most trusted and closest officials.

Nehemiah received a report about his native land: *Israel lays in ruin.* While some descendants of the original tribes of Israel had returned to their homeland, they lived in broken-down ghost towns, with no defenses against raids from neighboring clans. This news distressed Nehemiah. The burden of the Dream God placed within Nehemiah caused this once-joyful servant of the King to become dejected. King Artaxerxes took note of this and asked Nehemiah about the change in his demeanor.

Nehemiah explained the conditions of his homeland, Israel, and the dangers his people faced, to the king. Artaxerxes asked Nehemiah what his wish was for Israel. Nehemiah offered a bold Dream of rebuilding Jerusalem, the capital city of Judah and Israel. To not only rebuild the temple and the city, but also its walls so it could become a stronghold for the region. The king gave him the permission to attempt his Dream and gave him materials and a title to carry the Dream out. Nehemiah had added a powerful member to his team.

Nehemiah had traveled through the three first gates of the Dreamer's Quest: Dream Gate, Believe Gate and now the Dare Gate. He now needed to Dare to face the politics back in Jerusalem, and to face the enemies of Jerusalem. But most important, he needed to trust his plan and skills to get this done.

There were three phases to his plan: 1) rebuild the wall, 2) rebuild the structures within the wall, and 3) repopulate the city. The key to success was to quickly rebuild the wall so the next two phases could happen in safety. Critics said it could not be done. This wall was a huge structure, nearly forty feet high and about eight-and-a-half feet thick. It was about two-and-a-half miles long with thirty-four watchtowers and seven main gates.

Nehemiah recruited every family in Jerusalem to rebuild a small section of the wall near their house. Nehemiah instructed each family to divide the workforce into two groups. The first group was builders. The second group would stand guard over the first group with weapons, to protect them from raids.

What seemed an impossible task was completed in 52 days. This was in the face of enemies from all sides—Samaritans, Ammonites, Arabs, and Philistines. Next the gates were hung. Then people were "drafted" from the countryside to move into the city. As the population grew, rebuilding within the walls continued. Nehemiah was able to return to his former post: he had not only secured his Dream, but he had enlisted a team to support, build, and protect it. The Dream God had given to Nehemiah was now entrusted to the team.

You don't need to be a biblical scholar to understand that the Old Testament is the story of God's blessing upon a family, tribe, community, and nation that God wanted a personal relationship. What you may not know is that this story is revealed anew in the New Testament.

In the New Testament, God continues his attempt to have a personal relationship with his creation by living among us as one of us. The Gospel accounts record the birth and the life of this child named Jesus. He performed many miracles, which are documented for us today. During his life on earth, he devoted Himself to a band of followers that become known as his disciples. It would fall to them to spread the good News of Jesus Christ to the world.

The nation of Israel was blessed by God. God fulfilled the promise of a savior. That savior came from the lineage of Abraham, Isaac, and Jacob—and then, later, Boaz, David, and on through to Joseph and Mary. However, Israel rejected Jesus, the Promised One who was the Son of God. Being innocent of any crime, wrongdoing, or even a hint of sin, the Jewish officials plotted to have him killed.

Jesus was accused, tried, convicted, and executed. However, God knew before creation that His Son, Jesus, would be rejected. But God had a much greater purpose in mind for the death of Jesus. As a sacrifice for all the wrongs of mankind, Jesus was crucified, buried, and rose on the third day, securing victory over death.

Jesus appeared to many people for forty days after His resurrection. He then ascended to heaven before the disciple's eyes. The bulk of the New Testament is then devoted to the expansion of God's chosen people to include the entire world. This was to be accomplished by the building of the Church. It is prophesied in the New Testament that there will be followers from every tribe in the world.

From the small beginnings of a band of eleven followers, (after one of the twelve betrayed Jesus and hanged himself), a worldwide movement was begun. After another forty days of waiting after Jesus' ascension to be empowered by the Holy Spirit, who was sent to spark a worldwide movement, they broke free from their hiding place and proclaimed the message of Jesus to all who would listen. That first day of proclamation, the church grew from a small remnant of faithful followers to over 3,000 believers.

The last directives that Jesus gave the disciples before being caught up into heaven was a commission to spread the good news about a Savior for the world.

"Go...make disciples of all nations..."

Matthew 28:19

...He commanded them not to leave Jerusalem, but to wait for the Father's promise... "But you will receive power when the Holy Spirit has come on you, and you will be my witnesses in Jerusalem in all Judea and Samaria, and to the ends of the earth."

Acts 1:4b, 8

Jesus is the Creator I have spoken about so many times in this book. He is the one who has designed you for the Dream He has planted within your soul. His marching orders are as follows: While you are going (living your daily life within the story that I wrote for you), gather others to follow the Dream that I have placed within them.

- Make disciples by guiding them to Awaken to their Dream within—*to see with clarity* the Dream of the Creator.

- Help them to Believe by teaching them to *observe with competence* the new rules of life within their Dream.

- Encourage them to Dare to live within their Dream by *mastering with confidence* the life Jesus has given them.

- Inspire those new disciples to Do the activities they are designed to *execute with excellence*. This will result in *influence and impact* on a world blind to their Dreams within. By Awakening others to their Dreamer's Quests, they will not only fulfill their Dream, but inspire others to fulfill their Dreams.

Building your team, tribe, or community is the ultimate goal of the land beyond the Do Gate. Building your team is not just sharing your message and recruiting people. You build your team by adding clarity, competence, and confidence within each member. As you make imparting your Dream part of the fabric of your team's identity, you will be blessed by the Dreams of each person in the team. Your team will be strengthened by the gifts of each member of your tribe.

* * *

It is in the unexpected moments of clarity, competence, and confidence that I realize I am impacting my world. I realize that I am loving my life and I am living my legacy. It is an Awakening! It is a realization that I was made for this movement. I am the right person, in the right place, at the right time, with the right message to make an impact upon my world. While the influence and impact may not be shaking the world, they are deeply felt within my soul and the souls of those I serve.

The awareness that I am making a difference may come while I am speaking with a group, or to an individual, and I see the light turn on in their eyes. It comes when I tell my story of my journey and encourage them to step into their own Dreamer's Quest. It comes when I teach them about their new life within the Dreamer's Quest, and they gain the competence needed to really believe. It comes when I stand beside them in the face of fierce opposition to their Dream—whether from within or without—and give them courage to keep moving forward. Or, the moment may come as we work together, fulfilling our Dreamer's Quests and serving each other.

Your team is not only part of your journey—it becomes part of your destination. As you Awaken to the Dream your Creator has given you, you Awaken to the team that has surrounded you your whole life. There is also an Awakening to the team you will attract as you begin to live the life you are designed to live.

Many of my success stories depend upon others living their own Dreamer's Quests. Some of their stories spill over into my story. Like my dad's Awakening inspiring my own Awakening. My family and friends supporting and loving me. My teachers, coaches, and mentors guiding me. The pastors, authors, speakers, and thought leaders who have inspired me to attempt great things. It has taken a huge community of people to dig out the gold buried deep within my soul. I am in the debt of so many people who have gone before me. It is beyond my comprehension to express just how far back it goes.

* * *

THE DREAMER'S JOURNAL

Have you heard of Dr. Mordecai Ham of Louisville, Kentucky? He has a great story that very well has had an impact upon yours. Ham was born in 1877, in Allen County, Kentucky, a post-Civil War community. He was the descendant of eight generations of Baptist preachers. From a young age, he considered himself to be a Christian. He believed that one day he, too, would enter the ministry. In 1896, he entered business in Chicago. However, in 1900, he closed his business and devoted himself to full-time Christian ministry.

He was known for his fiery preaching, and he was not ashamed to delve in politics while preaching. Denouncing the use of alcohol, he zealously supported the Eighteenth Amendment to the U.S. Constitution. Again, in 1928, though most of his congregation was Democrats, he supported

Republican Herbert Hoover because the Democrat candidate was a Roman Catholic.

He became a traveling evangelist and radio speaker. From 1901 to 1941, he led 289 meetings in 22 states, which produced 303,387 professions of faith in Christ. At his revival meetings, he would end his lengthy sermons by giving a just-as-lengthy alter call. He would ask attendees to come to the stage and pray to receive Jesus Christ and of repentance from their sins.

It was at one of these meetings in Charlotte, North Carolina in 1934 that two young boys attended Dr. Ham's revival meetings. They did not like the way the preacher pointed directly at them when he denounced various sins, so they decided to return and sit in the choir behind the preacher, even though they could not sing. Their logic was that the preacher couldn't point in their direction if they were behind him.

After one of these meetings, one of the young boys said he was done and he was not coming back again. But he could not sleep all night, nor could he stop thinking about the message. The next night, the two boys arrived early and took their place as non-singing choir members. At the end of the service, a man approached them and said, "Come on, let's go up front."

That night, Billy Graham accepted Jesus Christ as his personal savior, and Grady Wilson dedicated his life to Christian service. Billy Graham later recalled in an interview that, at the first service, he was impressed with the size of the crowd and the "fight" the preacher had. That night, Billy Graham joined a new team. He set out on a lifelong Quest for a new Dream. He found a new mentor and was confronted with new rules. He learned to dare and do the impossible—reach the world with the gospel of Jesus Christ.

Who should we give credit to founding the team known as The Billy Graham Evangelist Association? Billy Graham? Grady Wilson? Or was it Dr. Mordecai Ham? One could certainly trace Dr. Ham's influence on Billy Graham. But wait, what about Dr. Ham's father, Tobias Ham, who was a Baptist preacher? Well, wait a minute—what about the line of eight Baptist ministers who preceded Tobias Ham?

This is the beauty of building your team. Your Awakening could be multiplied by Awakening the Dreamer's Quest within another, who will be used to Awaken another . . . I'm sure that, in the line of eight Baptist ministers, none of them could have ever imagined being summoned for meetings with world leaders and the president of the United States. Neither could they have had the foresight that one day, because of their influence, a person on their team would lead 417 crusades in 185 countries and territories on 6 continents with 215 million people in attendance.

What if just one of those Baptist ministers had broken that chain of eight? What if Dr. Ham had stayed in business in Chicago? What if Billy Graham had stayed away from the meetings because he didn't like getting a finger pointed in his direction? How different would our world be today?

We call it "the butterfly effect," and we have been confronted with this thought before. It is the basic tenet of the classic movie *It's a Wonderful Life*. We have sayings like, "There are no small roles, only small actors."

The world is waiting for you to Awaken to your Dream, to take your spot within your story. You may think you don't have anything to offer, that you could never make a difference. We don't even have the names of the eight generations of preachers that went before Dr. Mordecai Ham, who influenced the greatest evangelist the modern world has ever known. Which one of them was insignificant?

My dad, Charles Hershel Johnson, had an eighth-grade education. His family was so poor that they had to send him away to be cared for by the government. Was he insignificant? My mom, Callie Moore Johnson, had a sixth-grade education. She was the daughter of a sharecropper who never owned a house or a car. Was she insignificant?

My mom would pray with me at bedtime. One night, she explained to me that I needed to ask Jesus into my heart, and she helped me to pray the Sinner's Prayer. My dad made sure I was baptized and that I knew right from wrong. He studied and made changes in his life to live as an example to me.

My parents Awakened to the Dreams within them. They built their team—their family and their church. They did the best they could with what they had. They always wanted to spend a little more time with their sons and their families, they always wanted to see another person come to Christ, and they always wanted you to attend their church. My mom loved to cook. That was part of her Dream, to feed you. My dad loved to tell the story of Jesus. That was part of his Dream. He wanted to include you in what he believed was the greatest gift he ever received—a personal relationship with Jesus Christ. They had their flaws, but they also had Awakened to their Dreams. They built their team. Their influence and impact lives on today.

I'm living proof of that.

PART 5

To Be—Achieving!

Tripp has just returned from an outing to the lands he traveled many years before. His exploration beyond the gates of Dream, Believe, Dare, and Do have given way to discovery and innovation. He is now a permanent resident of New Ordinary. He finds joy from guiding others to their place in New Ordinary. With each Quest back through the gates, Tripp learns more details about his Dream. He learns that he has a passion to reveal the Dream Gate to the citizens of Ordinary. And what really excites him is that he now sees that his Dream is to guide others through the five gates that he has discovered.

Tripp becomes a guide for those who live in Ordinary almost by accident. He was traveling through Ordinary to revisit the Dream Gate. He was interrupted by a resident of Ordinary who wanted to know where he was heading. It reminded him of his first encounter with Alva many years before. As he looked into the eyes of this stranger, he could see his old self longing for a truth that always seemed to elude him. From that day, he has been on the lookout for others seeking answers.

At first, it feels like he is intruding into the lives of the masses of people in the city he once called home. But as he gains more understanding about his Dream, he learns the importance of disrupting the lives of those numbed by Ordinary. People who need to be shaken awake so they can Dream with their eyes wide open.

Tripp learns that the Creator not only has designed him for greatness, but that He has done the same for every living person. Tripp becomes conscious that his place is to serve the citizens of Ordinary. To serve them means to personally assist them in their Awakenings, to guide them into their transformations into the people the Creator designed them to be—to guide them to their true homes.

As he learns to serve the needs of those be meets on his journeys, he realizes that there are people all around him who are a perfect match for his skill set. It is no burden to assist these people, because it is what he was made for; it is his Dream. The pain that he once felt, he finds in many he encounters in Ordinary. The numbing effects of the routines of Ordinary he had to conquer are the same battle his new followers need to learn. In moments of clarity he realizes that he is made for this.

If he does discover a need he is not equipped to meet, one of his fellow citizens of New Ordinary, or one of his tribe, is a perfect match for that person and need. As his tribe of fellow Dream Questers—those that Tripp has guided through the gates—grows, so does the diversity of the needs Tripp encounters, and so do the numbers of those involved in the rescue efforts within Ordinary. With this involvement comes even more Quests to be embarked upon, Dreams to be filled, and even more people to be served with each passing day.

Tripp's impact is expanding beyond his wildest expectations. But then again, so is his Dream itself. His Dream has grown to a point that it no longer looks like it did when he first saw it just inside the Dream Gate. It would have terrified him to see the expanded version of his Dream the first time he gained clarity to see his Dream. But now, with each new repeated trip through the Dream, Believe, Dare, Do, and Be Gates comes a rush of excitement and joy of new insight and discovery.

His Dream is now his legacy. It is an expression of his love for the Creator and for all he encounters. He is always present, living in the activity, love, and joy of each moment. Life has deep meaning, and it brings great joy every day he spends within The Dreamer's Quest.

He is loving his life and living his legacy every moment of every day.

13

LOVING YOUR LIFE AND LIVING YOUR LEGACY TODAY!

The greatest legacy one can pass on to one's children and grandchildren is not money or other material things accumulated in one's life, but rather a legacy of character and faith.

Billy Graham

* * *

I never knew my grandpa on my dad's side or my grandma on my mom's side. I had met my dad's mother a couple of times, but each encounter ended poorly. Our last visit ended with grandma pulling a gun on my dad. She passed away when I was very young. My grandpa on my mom's side passed while I was in high school. Our relationship with Mom's side of the family wasn't much better than our relationship with Dad's side. I only saw Grandpa five or six times. Each visit was brief.

Getting to know Sandy's grandparents was a treat that I don't think anybody in her family really understood. What a heritage she had.

On her dad's side, Grandpa and Grandma had lived next door to Sandy her whole life. Grandpa was a recently retired mechanic, and Grandma was a homemaker. He had been a dirt track car driver and mechanic for a racing team in Indiana. He also had been a song leader for a traveling evangelist. I was so impressed with him. I would always try to get him to tell stories! Grandma was always in her kitchen, making something special for the family, while I sat in the living room listening to stories.

While there was a great deal of influence and impact from those grandparents, there was a visit with Sandy's grandparents on her mom's side that really impacted my life. Her grandfather was a retired milkman. (Now, some of you don't have any idea what that is. Back in the old days, you would have your milk delivered to your house before breakfast, along with eggs and cheese. No midnight runs to the Quickie Mart back then.) He could build just anything you could name. At least, that's how I remember it. He had a home on Lake Huron that was filled with his handiwork. You could look out their front window and watch ships sail by. He was a master at games. Euchre was his game of choice. You never wanted to lay the wrong card in his presence!

The most important thing I could say about him is that he was a godly man. He loved Jesus, and that shined out of him onto everybody he met. While there are many stories about his walk with Jesus that I missed out on, I was privileged to experience an Awakening moment because of him.

I had asked Sandy to marry me. Of course, I had to ask her dad for her hand in marriage and after several hours, I got approval to move forward with our plans. The approval came with the instruction that I should also speak with both sets of grandparents to get insight from each one of them.

Grandpa-down-the-hill was easy. A short trip, literally down the hill, and the conversation was complete. But Grandpa Erwin lived way up north near Cheboygan. This would have to be an overnight trip. I was a bit nervous about this, but I loved Sandy, so we made plans to be with them for a weekend.

After dinner one evening before playing cards, Grandpa Erwin invited me into the living room beside the wood-burning stove for a chat—just the two of us. He began to probe me with questions that very few people had ever asked me. "Phil, what do you really want in life?" he asked. "And why do you want it?"

Not *What do you plan to do?* or *What job are you hoping to do get?* He had asked me a question that I had never considered before. It caused me to stop and think, *What is the desire of my heart?*

I quickly popped off the same answer I had given my father-in-law to his question of "How do you plan to support my daughter?" Equally important question, but very different.

I said, "I plan to be a youth pastor, sir."

"Hmm, that's interesting. But what do you want in life?" he replied.

I was caught flat-footed. I thought I had answered him. I sat thinking for a moment. "I want to become a youth pastor that can point teens to Jesus?" I was hoping I was giving the "right" answer. I was getting closer, but I still didn't really hear what he was asking.

He sat there, looking me over with his half smile. He looked like he was either going to break out in a speech or in laughter, but he hadn't decided which yet. He let me stew a few more seconds. Sandy and grandma had moved to another room, but were trying to listen in on our talk. I could feel the pressure to get this right, not just for my sake but for Sandy's.

Grandpa broke the silence. "What I mean is this: what is your heart's desire, Phil? Is there a church you want to serve in? What do you want to see happen when you go to that church? What is your passion?"

His clarification caused me, for the first time, to gain clarity about what I really wanted to do with my life. It began to pour from me in a giant wave of words. It was the first time I declared to anybody other than Sandy what I believed my passion was.

"I want to make a difference. I want to make an impact, to give others not just what I have been given—the encouragement to do something with my life, the training to know Jesus—but even more than that. I want to guide them to experience life! A life they only dream of. The life that Jesus intended for them! I want to give them what I have been given, and even more, what Jesus has given them," I said in rapid fire. I heard myself saying the words, but at that time, I didn't know where they came from.

Grandpa Erwin sat quietly as I talked in excited tones. Then something quite unexpected happened. He got even more excited than I did. He talked in an excited, high-pitched voice, declaring a blessing over me. He declared that my Dream would be a reality in my life. I had been encouraged before, but never had I been blessed. I knew in that moment that I was being set apart for a special blessing. That blessing was coming directly from heaven to me.

That day I set my foot on my Dreamer's Quest. The clarity I received that evening mapped my path to see me through dark wilderness wanderings that I would soon begin to face. I became totally and radically committed to the cause of Jesus Christ again, this time with a mentor who would guide me along the way. The Creator's cause was now my cause! I owned it for myself. In that moment, I loved my life, and I was going to live my legacy beginning that day.

* * *

Joshua had devoted his entire adult life to serving God and his nation, Israel. His Dream was to live in the Promised Land God had given Abraham many years before. Joshua's first leadership position was as a young general, defending the Children of Israel's rear ranks when they were being raided by the Amalekites in Rephidim (Exodus 17:8-16).

He next took the position of Moses' assistant. He accompanied Moses up to Mount Sinai to receive the Ten Commandments. It was Joshua who first heard the celebration taking place when Aaron made the golden calf for the Israelites to worship. After Moses confronted the people and their sin, he entered the Tent of Meeting to face God on behalf of the people. Joshua also entered the Tent of Meeting, and remained there while Moses returned to the Israelite camp.

Later Joshua was appointed as one of the twelve spies who entered the Promise Land (Numbers 13:16-17). He and Caleb reported that the land flowed with milk and honey, and that God would give the land into the hands of Israel (Numbers 14:22-24). Instead of seeing the giants in the land, they saw the promise God had given them that they would occupy the land.

The people listened to the majority report of giants, and they turned away from entering the Promise Land. Joshua and Caleb would be the only adults who remained alive to enter the land forty years later. At the passing of Moses, Joshua was appointed to succeed him as leader of Israel.

Joshua led the Children of Israel across the Jordan River to occupy the land promised to them. After victory in the Battle of Jericho, Joshua led Israel to the small city of Ai, where they were soundly defeated. When he discovered the sin of Achan, one of the soldiers during the battle at Jericho, Joshua renewed Israel's commitment to God and led his forces to victory in a second battle of Ai.

Next, the Israelites were confronted by an alliance of five Amorite kings who controlled the major cities within the region. During this campaign, there was a fierce battle at Gibeon. Joshua saw that if he had more time, he could win the day. In a bold move, Joshua prayed for the impossible—for God to stop the sun in the sky so the Israelites could finish off their enemies.

So the sun stood still,
and the moon stopped,
till the nation avenged itself on its enemies,

as it is written in the Book of Jashar.

The sun stopped in the middle of the sky and delayed going down about a full day. There has never been a day like it before or since, a day when the LORD listened to a human being. Surely the LORD was fighting for Israel!

Joshua 10:13-14

After this battle, Joshua was able to secure most of the land promised to the Israelites. He was also able to allocate parcels of the land to each of the tribes of Israel. He established the Israelites, taking them from a nomadic tribe wandering in the wilderness to residents of the land given to their forefathers. The Dream given to Abraham, Isaac, and Jacob had now become a reality.

Joshua was about to die. He called the nation together one last time in Shechem. He had two items left to accomplish before he passed into eternity.

First, Joshua led the Israelites one last time to make a commitment to follow God and to remain faithful to Him and the Dream He had placed before the nation of Israel by way of the promises to their forefathers. Joshua admonished them to not turn back to the rules they had lived under in bondage to other gods. When the Israelites proclaimed that they would only serve God, Joshua challenged them that they couldn't do it. The people came back with even stronger resolve to trust God and to remain faithful to God alone. Then Joshua blessed them.

The second reason for meeting in Shechem was a final act to complete the return to the land promised to Israel. Joshua had the bones of Joseph buried in Shechem. The legacy of Abraham, Isaac, and Jacob was entrusted to Joseph, who saved the nation by moving them to Egypt. Then along came Moses, who had a special role to return Israel to the Promised Land. Moses took the people as far as the Jordan River, then passed leadership to Joshua.

That legacy was now passed to Joshua, who restored the nation to its birthright. By doing this, he completed the legacy of Moses and Joseph. Joshua was in the nation of Israel, who had a shared Dream to return to the land promised by God. It became a shared legacy that they passed along to each leader.

God-given Dreams are really the meaning of life. These Dreams are more than wishes for something we want. The Dreams are prophetic glimpses of our legacy. Our part may seem small at the time, but it is vital not only to your joy and peace in life, but to those who have gone before you and those who will follow.

* * *

It was a wonderful Thanksgiving celebration. Sandy and I had proudly presented our two daughters to our families. The image I remember most from that holiday was Grandpa Erwin holding my oldest daughter, who just turned one, on his lap. Grandma held our newborn daughter in her arms. Grandpa spoke to his great-granddaughter, then bragged about her to the other family members nearby. The flash of cameras went off as Grandpa held his little angel.

Little did we know that, just hours later, Grandpa would slip into eternity. The drive back north to his cottage on Lake

Huron would prove to be his final trip. His funeral was more of a celebration of life—a tribute to a man who had Awakened to the Creator's purpose for his life. Like my father, he was an extraordinary, ordinary man.

People shared stories of tribute to a life spent in service to God, family, and friends. One person shared that Grandpa had helped build the walls of that church. Many that day spoke of the personal impact this man had upon their lives. I remembered the blessing I had received from this man of God. I wept.

I'm not sure if a speaker placed this thought in my mind, or if the Holy Spirit whispered it to my soul, but I became consumed with a passion within my soul that day. It was now up to me to carry on Grandpa's passion . . . his love . . . his Dream. I have tried to tell people, over the years, what an impact Grandpa made on me, even though I had so few encounters with him.

I have often thought about how I could serve God, my family, my church, and my friends the way Grandpa Erwin did. I love Christmas, I think, because Grandpa loved Christmas so much. I love giving gifts to those close to me that stretch my limits, just like Grandpa did. I love making things to give to my children, just like Grandpa did. I love giving a family member or friend my undivided attention while we play a game or sit and talk together, just like Grandpa did.

I love my life when I am living my legacy. I love the victories that are won when I step over my Jordan River into my Promised Land. I love my life when I make my home within the boundaries of that Promised Land, and I live each day possessing my Dream.

When we truly own our Dream, the Dream the Creator has designed for us, and we cross over into and to occupy that Dream, we not only find fulfillment for ourselves, but we complete and continue the Dreams of those who have gone before us and those who will came after us. We are joining with a great tribe of people who are on the same Quest to fulfill their destinies in life. We are serving one another to achieve much more than we ever could alone.

Come on over into the Promised Land! Venture beyond the ordinary life that the world is pressuring you to live in.

- Fill the emptiness within your soul with the *Awakening to the Dreamer's Quest*.

- Replace your thirst for knowing with *belief in truth*.

- *Master* your fears with *daring confidence* to win the victories over obstacles.

- Discover your meaning in life by doing the impossible, with God's help.

Dream! Believe! Dare! Do! Be . . .

Pursue your intended purpose!
Imagine freedom from Ordinary!
Claim victories over obstacles!
Achieve the fulfillment of your legacy!
Awaken to your Dreamer's Quest.

ACKNOWLEDGEMENTS

MY HEROES: THOSE EXTRAORDINARY, ORDINARY PEOPLE WHO INSPIRE ME

My wife Sandy and daughters Jessica, JoAnna, Jenna, Julia, and Jala, who traveled with me on my Dreamer's Quest. They encouraged, challenged, and worked with me to reach my Dream.

My dad and mom, Charles Hershel and Callie Moore Johnson, who gave me everything they had to give.

My brothers, Chuck and Dave Johnson, who guided me to Dream for the very first time.

Grandpa and Grandma Erwin and Grandpa and Grandma Sanders, who became my examples of faith.

The Champaign family, who taught me courage.

MY MENTORS, TEACHERS, COACHES AND LEADERS IN MY DREAMER'S QUEST

Rev. Bob Richardson, Rev. Al Tedder, Pastor Bob Gevette, Pastor Roger Singleton, Ed Melberg, Karl Bairden, Dr. Dan Stevens, Dr. Ron Chadwick, Dr. Ron Meyers, Rev. Gene

Klingler, Rev. Gordon Lindsay, Rev. David Allen, Rev. Ric Joline, Rev. Jay Diller, Rev. Rev. Jim Custer, Kary Oberbrunner, Dr. Rodger Hall, Rev. Tony Web, Rev. Ed Lewis, Rev. Jim Auspruger, Rev. Paul Mutchler, Rev. Tom Maharis, Duke Heller, Dr. David Plaster, Dr. Gilbert Peterson, Dr. David Uth, Pastor Chris Ogden, the staff of Oakland Christian School from '71 to '78, the staff of Cornerstone University from '78 to '82, the Sonlife Training Team, the CE National/ Momentum Staff, Charis Fellowship, the New York Gospel Outreach team, and the sea of authors, speakers, pastors, and trainers I have encountered on my Dreamer's Quest.

MY TEAM: PARTNERS IN MY DREAMER'S QUEST

Jim and Linda Augspurger, Rick and Mindy Barlow, Josh and Becky Barlow, Charles and Ruth Bartlett, Karl and Fran Beaudry, Dennis and Stacey Beck, Mike and Vickie Blackwell, Ron and Cheri Boehm, Eric and Kristine Bowling, Charles and Betty Boyer, Kevin and Ulrike Brennan, Mervin and Dona Brenenan, Ron and Naomi Buffington, Calvary Church (Lancaster, PA), Roger and Pauline Campbell, Judy Carter, Kirk and Kay Carver, Tom and Gay Cathers, Jimmy and Vickie Chalmers, Doug and Michelle Champagne, Jack and Terri Chapin, Delia Clark, John and Joyce Clarke, Ron and Pam Clegg, Jon and Julia Coleman, Brian Collins, Columbus Grace Brethren Church, Carl and Macy Cooke, Jim and Triceine Custer, Scott, Adam and Anna Davis, Bill and Jackie Davis, Mark and Jann Day, Dan and Jane Dennis, Ed and Mari Dezago, Ken and Jane Dickinson, Rose Dillman, Charles and Sue Dozer, Erik and Terrah Dubasak, Chad and Jen Dutka, Peter and Tiffany Edmonds, Steve and Julie Edmonds, Cory and Karen Estabrook, Don and Dorothy Farmer, Lenny and Jackie Ferguson, First Baptist Church of Orlando, Mike and Judy Fisher, Florida District of FGBC, Pat Forgash, Doug and

Debbie Forsythe, Troy and Missy Fraker, Larry and Deborah Geelhood, Spencer and Cindy Geisen, Go 2 Ministry, Grace Community Church (Fremont), Grace Community Missionary Fellowship, Chuck and Chris Grant, Martin Guerena, Gulfview Grace Brethren Church, Norm and Mary Lou Gunsolley, Randy and Carolyn Hadley, Dick and Rhea Hames, Rob and Carrie Harmon, Mallory Harrigan, Larry and Joan Heath, Duke and Wanda Heller, Horizon West Church, Mark and Cathy Hussong, Chuck and Marilyn Johnson, Dave and Fredonna Johnson, Hershel and Callie Johnson, Jerry and Cathy Johnson, Ric and Shirley Joline, Jeff and Kristi Jordan, Jim and Kathy Kanzeg, Tom and Cheryl Kaufman, Jim and Susanne Kessler, Bill and Joan Kline, Earle and Beverly Knowles, Sharney and Molly Koch, Phil and Nancy Korodi, Bob and Stephanie LaMonte, Mark and Cherie Lappen, Kim and Esther Laurell, Chuck and Linda Lawson, Don and Barb Lewis, Gordie and Melissa Lindsay, Mike and Jean Luddeni, Robert and Kathryn Malone, Jim and Evelyn Mason, Kathryn McCollister, Clifford and Lori McElfresh, Dave and Dorothy Merrill, Brian and Wendy Miller, Jerry and Barb Miller, Wes and Mavis Miller, Gordon and Deborah Moskal, David and Toni Musser, Robert and Barbara Musser, Paul and Linda Mutchler, Randall and Dana Nottingham, Randy and LuAnne Ohms, Ormond Beach Grace Brethren Church, William and Teela Patmon, Kevin and Pam Pinkerton, Chuck and Gina Pledger, Jim and Charlotte Poyner, Harold and Janet Rettstatt, Margaret Rice, Tom and Lisa Rich, Michael and Sandy Rickly, Mark and Randa Rineer, Tom and Kathi Rollins, Jim and Charlene Roloson, Billy Sanders, Jim and Dorothy Sanders, Jim and Kim Sanders, Dick and Sally Schmuck, Tim and Cindy Schutter, Michael Seemueller, Dan and Katie Shearer, Bernie and Sue Simmons, Ken and Marilyn Simmons, Barry and Sandy Smades, Christina Smith, Phillip and Irene Smith, Bill and Jean Snell, Clyde and Mary Ruth Solander, Mike and Linda Solander, John and Lindsey Spreadbury, Mike and Sheri

Stanley, Mark and Shari Starner, Jeff and Pam Stone, Sandy Stout, Jon and Amy Sutton, Alan and Becky Thederahn, Jim Thompson, Dave and Amy Tucker, Mark and Lori Vaas, Ron and Sue VanWinkle, Alan and Jae VanDyke, Tim and Kathleen Wagner, Craig and Cathy Watterson, Tony and Cathy Webb, Aaron Weiss, William and Ann Wheat, John and Jerry Whinnery, and Eric and Rebecca Whitney.

APPENDIX A

JOURNAL AND GROUP DISCUSSION QUESTION

PART 1: TO DREAM—AWAKENING!

- Did you identify with Tripp in any way?

- Does Ordinary sound like the place you live?

CHAPTER 1: AWAKENING YOUR DREAM! YOU ARE MEANT FOR GREATNESS

- As a child, what were your daydreams about your future? Are there clues in those memories about your Dream?

- What did your share with family and friends about your Dreams? What were their reactions?

- Did you fear sharing your Dream with others? Why or why not?

- Describe your identity without using terms that describe what you do (*mom, salesperson, teacher,* etc.).

- How does the idea that God created you personally (clicked your DNA together exactly how He wanted) affect what you believe about yourself and your future?

- What difference would it make in your life to have clarity about your Dream?

CHAPTER 2: AWAKENING YOUR DREAM! THE CALLING OF YOUR SOUL

- Have you ever been at a crossroads in your Dreamer's Quest? Which path did you choose? The path moving towards greater commitment? The path to greater clarity of your Dream? Or did you retreat to the land of Ordinary, where everyone is asleep, but never Dreams?

- As you become more aware of your Dream, have you experienced greater clarity? What has that been like for you?

- Describe how you feel when you are not pursuing your passion, purpose, and Dream. Is there emptiness, longing, or pain?

- Do you try to numb the negative feelings you experience when you are not in pursuit of your Dream? If so, how?

- Have you ever worked through your discontented longings?

- Who are your truth-tellers? Do they seek you out, or do you seek them out?

- As you begin your Dreamer's Quest, do you identify more with Jonah or Joseph?

CHAPTER 3: AWAKENING YOUR DREAM! THE CALLING OF TOTAL AND RADICAL COMMITMENT

- What is the cause that the Creator has written upon your heart?

- What clues from your childhood desires can help you discover how God has designed you? What desires of your heart do you see as guideposts for your Dreamer's Quest?

- Do you have any natural talents or abilities that could guide you toward your Dream?

- What challenges have you faced that have made you the person you are?

- What does "total and radical" mean to you today? Are you willing to go there?

PART 2: TO BELIEVE—ACQUIRING!

- Have you made the commitment to go for your Dream?

- Do you feel like you need more information to move forward?

CHAPTER 4: OBSERVING YOUR MIND: THE NEW PRINCIPLES DESIGNED FOR THE QUEST

- What do you believe about God?

- What do you believe about your Dream?

- Is there a relationship between your beliefs about God and your beliefs about your Dream?

- What waves and winds distract you from your Dream?

- Was there a time in your life when you let your circumstances derail your progress toward your Dream?

- Which is easier for you to believe in: your circumstances or your Dream?

- Do you really believe in your Dream?

CHAPTER 5: OBSERVING YOUR HEART: THE NEW PASSION MEANT FOR THE QUEST

- If there were something you could change about yourself, what would it be?

- What is the most embarrassing action you have willingly taken?

- If you could rewrite your childhood, what would you change and why?

- What do you believe about yourself when you read that "you are designed for greatness and to win?"

- Have you ever allowed yourself to become totally committed to something? If so, how did it impact your life? If not, why? What do you think you missed out on?

- Have you ever tried to do something out-of-the-box? How did that work out for you?

- Have you ever taken a leap of faith, only to find that it wasn't that big of a leap?

- What is holding you back from your Dream? What transformation do you need in your life today?

CHAPTER 6: OBSERVING YOUR SOUL: THE NEW PURPOSE INTENDED FOR THE QUEST

- What motivates you to action?

- Do you have a mentor?

- Do you smile often?

- Would others say you are a positive person?

- How can you use your Dream to help other people?

- Are you willing to give your Dream to others so they can benefit from it?

- Do you believe in win-win situations? Do you work to achieve them?

PART 3: TO DARE—AFFECTING!

- Are there well-intentioned critics in your life?

- What are your self-limiting beliefs?

CHAPTER 7: DARE TO DISCERN YOUR GATEKEEPERS: THE WELL-INTENTIONED CRITICS

- When you begin to act upon your calling, what images, words, or memories make you want to retreat back to Ordinary?

- Who opposes your commitment to the Dreamer's Quest? How do they oppose it? Do they have your best interest at heart, but allow fear to cloud their thinking? Is your example holding a mirror to their life?

- Do you dwell upon the negative things people say to you? Do you focus more on those messages than the messages the Creator has given you? Who is the gatekeeper of your soul?

- What battle scars have you received along your Dreamer's Quest? What scars would you receive if you let outside gatekeepers control your calling in life? Which pain would be greater?

- How will you become the gatekeeper of your Dream?

- How does Philippians 4:8 help you become a gate-keeper of your mind? ("Whatever is true, whatever is noble, whatever is right, whatever is pure, whatever is lovely, whatever is admirable—if anything is excellent or praiseworthy—think about such things.")

CHAPTER 8: DELETING YOUR SCRIPTS: THE FALSE SCRIPTS WE BELIEVE

- Monitor your self-talk by using Dr. Rodger Hall's alarm clock method.

- What patterns surface in your research of your self-talk habits?

- In what areas do you have positive self-talk habits?

- In what areas do you need to adjust your self-talk habits?

- What beliefs do you have about yourself that are true?

- What beliefs do you have about yourself that are false?

- What sources of negative input do you need to control or eliminate?

- What positive messages will you use to replace the false beliefs you have about yourself?

CHAPTER 9: DARE TO DIMINISH DETOURS: PERCEIVING YOUR PROBLEMS AS BLESSINGS IN DISGUISE

- Are you more of a victor or a victim?

- How will you limit the victim mentality and grow the victor mentality?

- What trials have helped to shape you into a positive person who makes an impact on the world?

- How do you (or can you) gain perspective about your trials?

- What trials in your life do you feel have been upgraded to testings? What positive outcomes have come from these tests?

- In what areas are you tempted to give up?

- What triggers you to plan your escape from pain?

- When do you give into temptation? When you begin to think about the escape? When do you allow yourself to be lured by the temptation?

- What would the death of your Dream look like? What are the consequences of the death of your Dream?

- Have you ever been able to press through pain to achieve peace and hope?

PART 4: TO DO – ACTIVATE!

- What does your team look like?

- Are you serving your team?

CHAPTER 10: AWAKEN YOUR LEGACY

- Have you experienced joy from serving others?

- What is the source of joy in your life? Who are you serving?

- Has the meaning of your Dream (or parts of it) remained hidden from you? Have you stayed faithful to the Dream anyway?

- What leads to a sense of joy and fulfillment in your life?

- Of your areas of excellence, which you would enjoy even if you were not paid to do them?

- How can you use those areas of excellence to serve others?

- How will you become more effective in using your skills?

CHAPTER 11: ACCOMPLISH YOUR CALLING

- How does your Dream serve others?

- Can you think of a time when you served others and felt a deep sense of fulfillment?

- Have you ever been tempted to use your Dream selfishly?

- How does service, caring, and giving relate to your Dream?

- How does selfishness, using, and taking relate to your Dream?

- How would your life change if you focused only on serving others with your Dream, not on fulfilling your desires?

CHAPTER 12: ASSEMBLE YOUR TEAM

- Have you ever felt fulfillment in your life?

- When did you recognize your Dream?

- What did your team look like as you began to discover the Dream your Creator had given you? Who were the influencers and impacters at that time?

- Are there members of your team you need to cut off or reduce contact with?

- Do you have a need for coaching to train you in an area? Do you need a mentor to guide you through one of the gates of the Dreamer's Quest?

- Who are you serving? How does the fulfillment of your Dream serve others?

- Which Gate do you need to revisit so you can have greater influence and impact within your team?

- Dream Gate: Clarity to See?

- Believe Gate: Competence to Observe?

- Dare Gate: Confidence to Master?

- Do Gate: Courage to Execute?

- How will you serve your team?

PART 5: TO BE—ACHIEVING!

- Is your life marked by joy?

- Do you love your life?

- Are you living your legacy today?

CHAPTER 13: LOVING YOUR LIFE AND LIVING YOUR LEGACY TODAY!

- Do you love your life and live your legacy every day?

- Are you present every day?

- Are you stretching your Dream? Are you content with where you are today?

- Are you guiding others to realize their Dreams?

ABOUT THE AUTHOR

Philip B. Johnson is dedicated to assisting others in discovering their purpose in life. Through his writing, speaking and coaching he helps individuals and organizations to achieve their Dream. His message of truth, hope, and confidence has impacted many. Phil's personal journey is an extraordinary story of an ordinary guy.

For years Phil struggled with the inconsistent messages that ran through his mind. He knew that he had a special purpose in life. However, he questioned if he had anything of value to offer in life. The magnitude of his Dream was greater than his evaluation of his abilities. It was his personal struggle with these questions that lead him to discover the answers to two of life's most important questions: *Am I enough?* and *Do I have enough?* These answers are now the foundation of his message.

His quest for answers has led him on a journey that has included ministries in five churches, founding and running a ministry on his own, starting three businesses, and living in five states. Phil also had opportunities to use the talent that God gave him in companies such as The Walt Disney Company, where he held positions of trainer and speaker to new hires.

Phil has served on several national boards. He has devoted his life to impacting as many people as possible by meeting, caring, and helping them to discover God's plan for their lives. He and his wife Sandy have five amazing daughters. You can connect with Phil at CoachingSome.org.

COMPARE ➜ COMPETE ➜ CREATE

Since the beginning of time, we've been gazing at our neighbor's lawn, trying to see whose grass is greener. Thanks to the internet we now have access to billions of backyards—at all hours of the day and night. But grass is no longer the focus. We've migrated to followers, dollars, and views.

* * *

Comparison is a popular blood sport, making causalities of us all. Our competition isn't found in the marketplace. It's found in the mirror. We don't need to change the world. We need to change ourselves. And somewhere in the process, we'll end up changing both.

* * *

You've been created to create, and it's time to admit that you're in a race of one. Marathons and mountaintops share one thing in common. Both are reached by taking YOUR NEXT BEST STEP.

Igniting Souls Conference

October 25-27, 2019 | Columbus, Ohio

This event has been SOLD OUT for the last four years!

Sign-up today!

https://vt226.isrefer.com/go/isc/YPCoach/

Your Next Best Step!

Join us at ...

The Dreamer's Quest

Live Events

Imagine: **The Dreamer's Quest live and in person.** We all learn differently, and many learn best in live settings. Studies show that engaging the senses allows the message to **transform our minds.**

Invest in your Dream...
Discover your Purpose ...

Awaken to the life you always knew you could have...

Take your path to ... ***Loving your Life and Living your Legacy ... Today!***

BRING PHIL INTO YOUR BUSINESS OR ORGANIZATION

AUTHOR, COACH, TRAINER, SPEAKER.

PHIL KNOWS THE TRUST THAT YOU GIVE TO OUTSIDE SPEAKERS AND TRAINERS WHEN YOU BRING THEM IN TO SHARE WITH YOUR TEAM. HE HAS BEEN IN YOUR SHOES. BEING A LEADER AND RUNNING HIS OWN MINISTRY FOR TEN YEARS, HE UNDERSTANDS THE NEEDS OF THE ORGANIZATION IS MORE IMPORTANT THAN THE NEEDS OF THE VISITING SPEAKER.

PHIL BRINGS 35+ YEARS OF EXPERIENCE IN READING THE NEEDS OF THE PEOPLE IN FRONT OF HIM AND DELIVERING THE RIGHT MESSAGE OF TRANSFORMATION. HE OFFERS THE FOLLOWING:

- **Coaching:** *The Dreamer's Quest is a deep dive into each of the five gates you must navigate to find the life you love and to live your legacy TODAY!*
- **Coaching Some Academy:** for convenience and cost, we offer online coaching in both The Deeper Path and The Dreamer's Quest.
- **Live Events:** Stay in contact with us to hear about our next live event.
- **Speaking Services:** Phil looks forward to coming to your next event to share his stories of transformation and hope.

CONTACT PHIL TODAY TO BEGIN THE CONVERSATION

Find out more about hosting a Dreamer's Quest live event:
Phil@CoachingSome.org

phil@coachingsome.org / www.coachingsome.org